GAMES

MAGAZINE Junior

Kids'
Big Book
of
Games

GAMES
MAGAZINE
Junior

Kids' Big Book of Games

EDITED BY KAREN C. ANDERSON

WORKMAN PUBLISHING, NEW YORK

Library of Congress Cataloging-in-Publication Data
Games junior kids' big book of games/edited by Karen C. Anderson
p. cm.
  Summary: Presents over 125 games, including picture puzzles, scrambled comics, riddle searches, logic defiers, memory contests, connect-the-dots, out-of-orders, mazes, crisscrosses, and rebuses.
  1. Indoor games–Juvenile literature. 2. Puzzles–Juvenile literature. [1. Games. 2. Puzzles]
1. Anderson, Karen, C. II. Games junior.
GV1223.G36 1990 793.73–dc20 89-40727 CIP AC
ISBN 0-89480-657-2

Book design by Mark Freiman

  Front cover illustrations: Train by Bob Rose; king and stamp by Mark Mazut; frog and fox by Holly Kowitt.
  Back cover illustrations: Teacup and cake by Mark Mazut; flipped coin by Ron Barrett; bus by Ted Enik.

Workman books are available at special discounts when purchased in bulk for premiums and sales promotions as well as for fund-raising or educational use. Special editions or book excerpts can also be created to specification. For details, contact the Special Sales Director at the address below.

Workman Publishing Company, Inc.
708 Broadway
New York, New York 10003

Manufactured in the United States of America
First printing, June 1990

20

The material in this book has previously appeared in GAMES Junior, which is a trademark of PSC Games Limited Partnership.

Introduction

GAMES magazine was started in 1977 and has been puzzling people ever since. Maybe you've seen it in a friend's or relative's house. If so, you're not alone: A lot of young people have seen it—and liked it. When the editors of *GAMES* heard that there were a great many kids out there who wanted a magazine of their own that was just like *GAMES*, we listened.

In July 1987, we tested *GAMES Junior* as a 16-page insert within *GAMES* Special Edition. The response was enthusiastic, and in October 1988 we launched *GAMES Junior* as a regular publication. We've been publishing it for two years now, and already it has become a favorite recreation at home and in the classroom.

Like *GAMES*, the primary goal of *GAMES Junior* is to provide entertainment by supplying innovative verbal, visual, and logic puzzles. We create games that we hope will challenge, amuse, and occasionally stump our readers. As an added attraction that parents and teachers like (but which you're not supposed to know), the puzzles in the magazine may enhance problem-solving abilities and improve language skills.

This book includes all of the puzzle types that you will find in *GAMES Junior* magazine, organized by chapter. There are connect-the-dots, what's-wrong-with-this-picture? puzzles, crosswords, riddle searches, mini mysteries in Detective's Notebook, magic tricks, games, and quizzes. The final chapter, Big Bad Toughies, contains challenging puzzles from all of the categories. The last puzzle, Seven Up!, was designed especially for this book. It consists of seven mini puzzles, which all need to be solved in order to find the answer to the overall puzzle.

So get to it! Sharpen some pencils and dig in!

Karen C. Anderson
Managing Editor

Contents

1

PICTURE PUZZLES 9

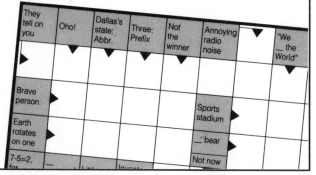

Sounding Off 10
Match-Up 1 .11
Connect-the-Dots 1. 12
Hide and Peek 13
Eyeball Benders 14
Match-Up 2 .15
Chair and Chair Alike. 16
Triangle Tangle 1 18
Highway Maze. 19
S Is for Saturday 20
Mixture Pictures 21
Connect-the-Dots 2. 22
Jungle Quest 23
Hats Off! 24
F Is for Farm 26
Triangle Tangle 2 27
What's Wrong With This Picture? 1 28
Connect-the-Dots 3. 29
Match-Up 3 .30
Back-to-School Maze 31
J Is for Junior's Room 32
Midnight Munchies 33
Hey Diddle Riddle 34
What's Wrong With This Picture? 2 35
Heads or Tails?. 36
Trick-or-Treat Maze 38
P Is for Pet Shop 39
Classroom Caper 40
Nature's Secrets. 41

Connect-the-Dots 4. 42
What's Wrong With This Picture? 3 43
C Is for Circus 44
Cabin Hideaway. 45
Christmas Maze. 46
Triangle Tangle 3 47
Feet First. 48
Assembly Line 50
Ice Tease 51
Match-Up 4 .52
Secrets of the Swamp. 53
Strange Happenings. 54
Whose Hues? 56

2

WORD PLAY 57

Picture Crossword 1. 58
Pencil Pointers 1 59
Spelling Beehive 60
Presidential Dessert. 60
Riddle Search 1 61
Disabled Vehicles 62
CAR Quiz. 62
Crisscross Puzzle 1 63
On the Double 64
Crossword Puzzle 1 65
From House to House. 66
Fill-Ins 1 67
Collectors' Items 68
Picture Crossword 2. 69
Pencil Pointers 2 70

They tell on you	Oho!	Dallas's state: Abbr.	Three: Prefix	Not the winner		Annoying radio noise	▼		"We __ the World"
▼		▼	▼	▼					
									▼
Brave person		▼							
					Sports stadium	▼			
Earth rotates on one						__ bear	▼		
7-5=2, for				Invent		Not now			

Sum Fun 71
Presto-Chango 71
Pet Rebuses 72
Crossword Puzzle 2 73
Riddle Search 2 74
Crisscross Puzzle 2 75
Mirror Message 76
Mixed Pairs 76
Now Hear This. 77
Alphabetically Speaking. 77
Crossword Puzzle 3 78
Body Building 79
Riddle Search 3 80

Picture Crossword 3 81
Crossword Puzzle 4 82
Word Wheel 83
PAN Handling 84
Here Hear! 84
Riddle Search 4 85
Riddle Acrostic. 86
Crisscross Puzzle 3 87
Pencil Pointers 3 88
Among the Flowers 89
Riddle Search 5 90
PuZZling Fill-Ins 91
Bumper Crop 91
Build-a-Word 92
Horsing Around 92
Crossword Puzzle 5 93
Proverbial Confusion 94
Fill-Ins 2 94
Riddlegrams 95
Seeing Things 96

3

GAMES & TRIVIA 97

Dinosaur Quiz 98
Dinosaur Eyeball Benders 99
Riddle Me This 100

Takeaway Games 101
The Olden Daze 102
Can You Guess? 104
Play Ball! 105
Which Came First? 106
Alaska? I'll Ask Ya! 108
What's in a Game? 110
States of Confusion 111
Who Was It? 112
Twelve Tough Teasers 114
Cats Incredible! 116
What's the Difference? 118
High-Low Quiz 119
Travel Bingo 120

4

MYSTERY, LOGIC & NUMBERS . . . 121

Out of Order 1 122
The Perfect Match 123
Detective's Notebook, Case 1 124
  Lip Reading 125

The Dating Game 126
Work Boxes 127
Out of Order 2 128
A Logical Treasure Hunt 129
Coin Return 130
What Comes Next? 131
Detective's Notebook, Case 2 132
  Pigpen Code 133
  Top Secret 133
Pack Magic 134
Out of Order 3 135
Color Schemes 136

Lights Out! 137
Out of Order 4 138
Triviarithmetic. 139
The Magic Die 140
Square Deal 141
The Magic Touch 142
Out of Order 5 143
Lizard Logic. 144

5

BIG BAD TOUGHIES 145

Cross Numbers. 146
Out on a Limb 146

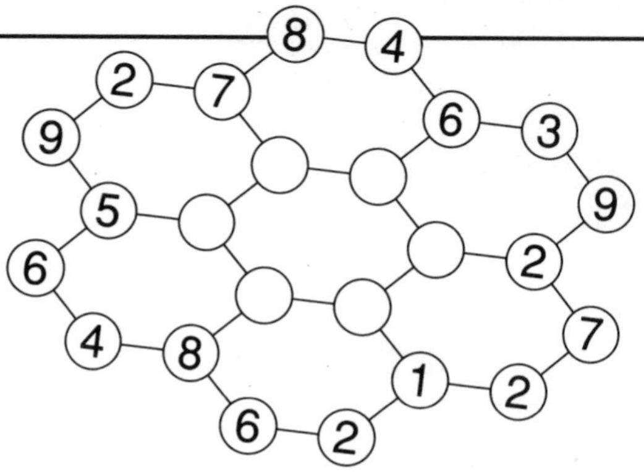

Magic Hex .147
Categories .147
Play by Number 148
Stately Names 149
Three-Sum. 150
Break It Up 150
Facts and Figures. 151
Seven Up! .152

6

ALL THE ANSWERS 155

1
Picture
Puzzles

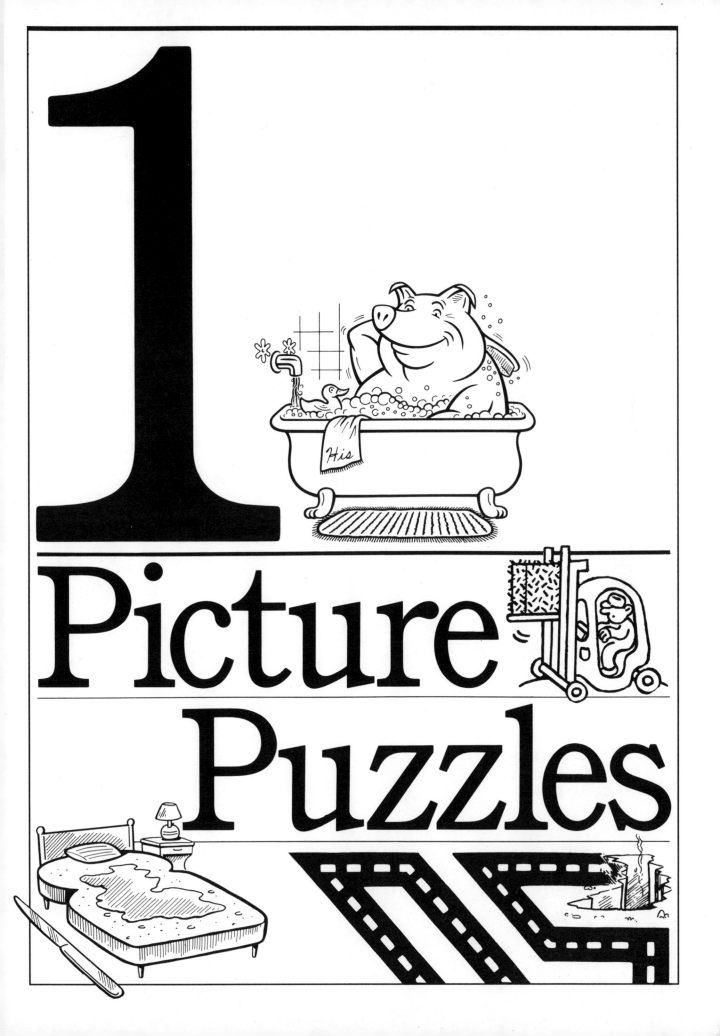

Sounding Off

The sounds that go with each of these pictures have been mixed up. Can you unscramble them by writing the correct sound under each picture?

Answers, page 156

1._____

2._____

3._____

4._____

5._____

6._____

7._____

8._____

9._____

PUZZLE AND ILLUSTRATION BY ROBERT LEIGHTON

GAMES

Match-Up 1

These six animal music groups look very similar, but only two are exactly alike. Can you find the two that match?

Answer, page 156

A   B

C   D

E   F

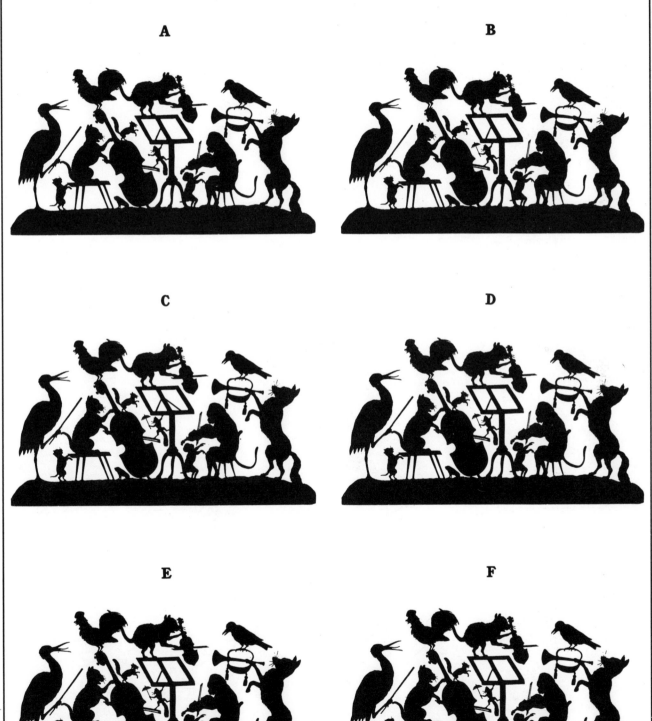

PUZZLE BY BARRY SIMON

Connect-the-Dots 1

Connect the dots in order from 1 to 65 to complete the picture.   *Answer, page 156*

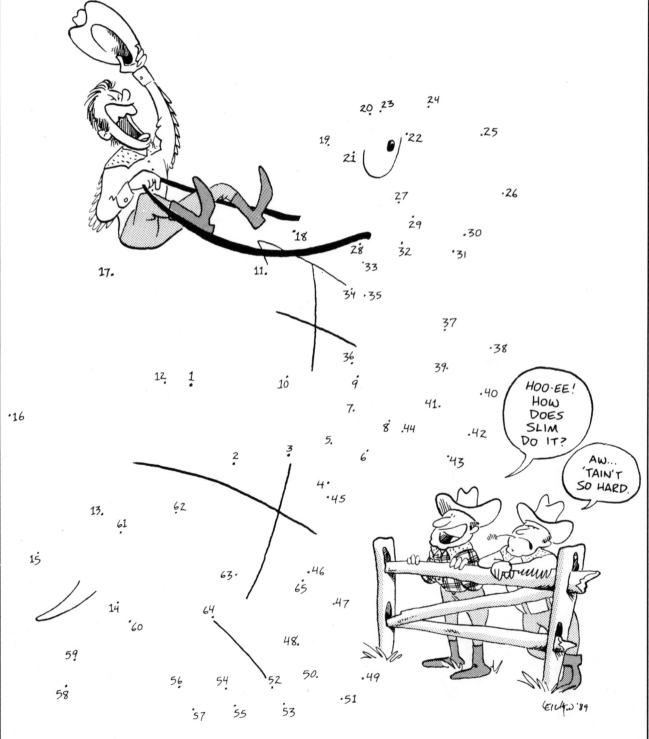

GAMES

Hide and Peek

Memory Test (Part One)

Junior and his friends are playing hide-and-seek and Junior is "it." Study the scene, as Junior is doing from the top of the stairs (he's peeking), for up to three minutes. Then turn the page to test your memory.

Hide and Peek

Memory Test (Part Two)
(PLEASE DON'T READ THIS UNTIL YOU HAVE READ PAGE 13.)

You probably know where all of the kids were hiding. But can you answer these other questions about the scene?

Answers, page 156

1. How many kids were hiding?
2. What was Junior holding?
3. What type of animal was the sculpture on the mantelpiece?
4. On the floor is some playing equipment for what two sports?
5. What was in front of the chair closest to the balcony?
6. Which of these portraits was not above the fireplace?

Eyeball Benders

Here are 5 close-up photographs of everyday objects. What are they?

Answers, page 156

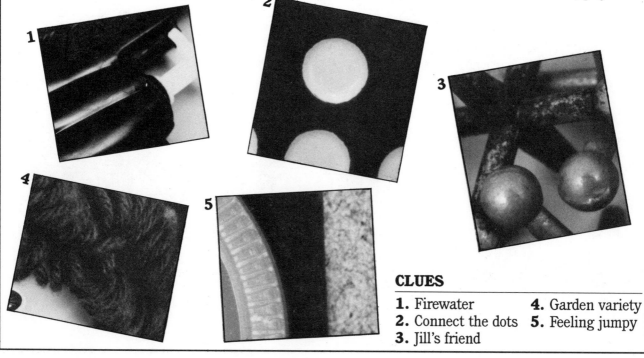

CLUES

1. Firewater
2. Connect the dots
3. Jill's friend

4. Garden variety
5. Feeling jumpy

PHOTOGRAPHS BY KEITH GLASGOW

Match-Up 2

These six gremlins look very similar, but only two are exactly alike. Can you find the two that match?

Answer, page 156

A   **B**   **C**

D   **E**   **F**

ILLUSTRATIONS BY ROBERTA L. COLLIER

G A M E S

Chair and Chair Alike

Each of these chairs has just been used by one of the people shown at the bottom. Can you match the chairs to the people?

Answers, page 156

E

F

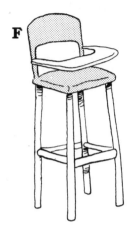

G

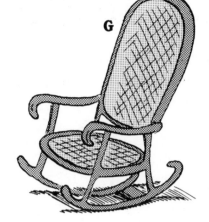

I

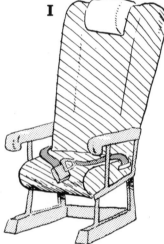

J

H

6

7

8

9

10

PUZZLE AND ILLUSTRATIONS BY ROBERT LEIGHTON

Triangle Tangle 1

Color in each area that has exactly three sides, and you'll see something you wouldn't want to play with.

Answer, page 156

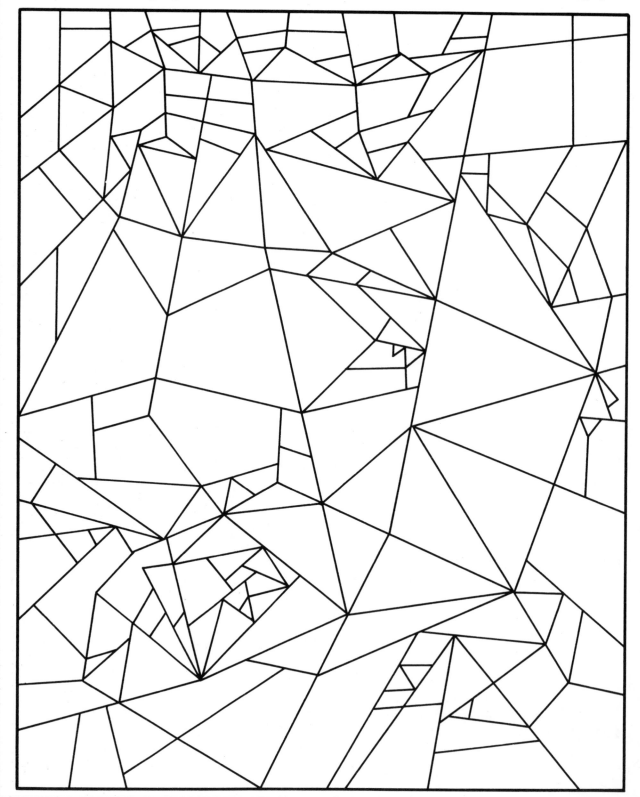

ILLUSTRATION BY MARK MAZUT

Highway Maze

Can you help the car at the bottom find its way to the airport in the upper right? You may travel over bridges and through tunnels, but you must avoid obstacles and you may not go off the road.

Answer, page 156

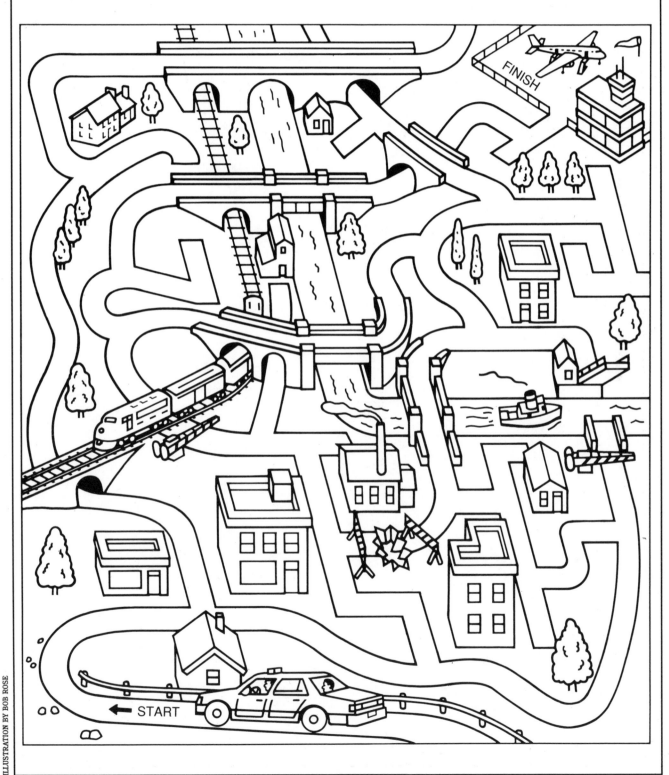

S Is for Saturday

How many things can you find in this scene that begin with the letter S?
Spotting at least 30 is skillful; 35 or more is sensational.

Answers, page 157

PUZZLE BY ANDREA CARLA MICHAELS/ILLUSTRATION BY ROBERT FRANK

Mixture Pictures

Each of these pictures can be described by a pair of words that rhyme. For example, the first picture shows a cart full of darts, or a DART CART. The first letters of the other answers are shown. How many can you figure out?

Answers, page 157

1. D A R T
C A R T

2. B _ _ _
C _ _ _ _

3. C _ _ _
J _ _

4. C _ _ _
H _ _ _

5. B _ _ _ _
B _ _ _

6. T _ _ _
P _ _ _

7. H _ _ _
N _ _ _

8. S _ _ _ _
S _ _ _ _ _

9. L _ _ _
S _ _ _ _

PUZZLE AND ILLUSTRATIONS BY MARK MAZUT

Connect-the-Dots 2

Connect the dots in order from 1 to 58 to find out what Junior is so afraid of.

Answer, page 157

OH NO! NOT **THAT!** ANYTHING BUT **THAT!**

PUZZLE AND ILLUSTRATION BY ROBERT LEIGHTON

Jungle Quest

Can you find the following things hidden in this jungle scene: bow tie, candle, comb, crown, cup, fish, fishhook, fork, glove, guitar, hammer, mitten, necktie, phone, rabbit, sock, toothbrush?

Answers, page 157

PUZZLE AND ILLUSTRATION BY MARK MAZUT

Hats Off!

Each of the eight people on the top of these two pages has traded hats with a person from the bottom of the page. Can you draw a line to connect each pair, and reunite each hat with the person it belongs to?

Answers, page 158

A   B   C   D

1   2   3   4

E

F

G

H

5

6

7

8

PUZZLE AND ILLUSTRATIONS BY MARK MAZUT

G A M E S

F Is for Farm

How many things can you find in this farm scene that begin with the letter F? Finding at least 20 is fair, 30 is fine, and 40 or more is fantastic.

Answers, page 157

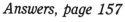

PUZZLE BY KAREN ANDERSON/ILLUSTRATION BY HOLLY KOWITT

Triangle Tangle 2

Color in each area that has exactly three sides, and you'll see something that's out of this world.

Answer, page 158

What's Wrong With This Picture? 1

Can you find at least 10 things wrong with this golfing scene? *Answers, page 158*

PUZZLE BY KAREN ANDERSON/ILLUSTRATION BY LORETTA LUSTIG

Connect-the-Dots 3

This connect-the-dots puzzle has pictures instead of numbers. Each picture begins with a different letter of the alphabet, and every letter of the alphabet is used once. Figure out what word each picture illustrates, then connect the dots in alphabetical order. The first line, going from the APPLE to the BASEBALL, has been drawn to get you started.

Answer, page 158

PUZZLE AND ILLUSTRATIONS BY ROBERT LEIGHTON

Match-Up 3

These six pictures look very similar, but only two are exactly alike. Can you find the two that match?

Answer, page 158

A

B

C

D

E

F

ILLUSTRATIONS BY MARK MAZUT

G A M E S

Back-to-School Maze

Can you help the new bus driver find the way to the school at the bottom?

Answer, page 158

ILLUSTRATION BY TED ENIK

J Is for Junior's Room

Can you find 20 or more things in this playroom whose names start with the letter J?

Answers, page 158

Midnight Munchies

Memory Test (Part One)

This is what you saw in the refrigerator before you went to bed. Study it for up to two minutes, then turn the page.

Midnight Munchies

Memory Test (Part Two)
(PLEASE DON'T READ THIS UNTIL YOU HAVE READ PAGE 33.)

As you are trying to go to sleep, you keep picturing all the good things waiting to be eaten in the kitchen. Which of these foods would you find in the fridge if you crept downstairs for a snack (assuming no one else has taken anything since you last peeked)?

Answers, page 158

Hey Diddle Riddle

Can you discover the riddle and its answer in the lines to the right? Hint: Tilt the page almost to eye level in order to read.

Answer, page 158

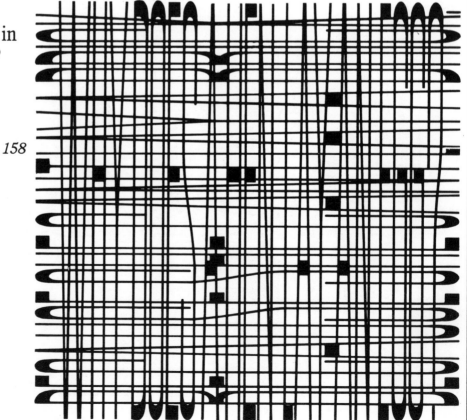

What's Wrong With This Picture? 2

Besides the fact that Spot just ate all of the hamburgers, can you find at least 10 mistakes in this backyard barbecue scene?

Answers, page 158

Heads or Tails?

This puzzle will have you tossing and turning. Can you match the faces on the animal coins below with their flip sides on the facing page?

Answers, page 159

PUZZLE BY ROBERT LEIGHTON/ILLUSTRATION BY RON BARRETT

GAMES

Trick-or-Treat Maze

Can you help the trick-or-treaters in the upper left find their way to the jack-o'-lantern full of candy in the middle? You may not go into the areas where there are bats.

Answer, page 159

ILLUSTRATION BY PAUL RICHER

P Is for Pet Shop

How many things can you find in this pet shop scene that begin with the letter P? Finding 20 is pretty good; 30 is practically perfect. *Answers, page 159*

Classroom Caper

Can you find 10 or more things wrong with this schoolroom scene?

Answers, page 159

PUZZLE BY KAREN ANDERSON/ILLUSTRATION BY TED ENIK

Nature's Secrets

Can you find the following things hidden in this meadow scene: banana, bowling pin, fish, glove, golf club, hairbrush, heart, horseshoe, mitten, needle, pair of dice, penny, sailboat, spider, streetlight, sword, umbrella, wishbone?

Answers, page 160

GAMES

Connect-the-Dots 4

Connect the dots in order from 1 to 70 to figure out what's in the air.

Answer, page 159

ILLUSTRATION BY ROBERT LEIGHTON

What's Wrong With This Picture? 3

Can you find at least 12 things wrong with this camping scene?

Answers, page 160

PUZZLE BY KAREN ANDERSON/ILLUSTRATION BY PHIL SCHEUER

GAMES

C Is for Circus

How many things can you find in this circus scene that begin with the letter C? Finding 25 or more is commendable; only the craftiest solvers will find at least 30.

Answers, page 160

Cabin Hideaway

Can you find the following things hidden in and around this log cabin: book, butterfly, cane, clothespin, comb, fin (swimming flipper), frying pan, golf tee, hammer, hat, jug, lollipop, pencil, pickle, ruler, scissors, ski, snake, umbrella?

Answers, page 161

GAMES

ILLUSTRATION BY MARK MAZUT

Christmas Maze

Can you find the way from the bedroom to the Christmas tree?   *Answer, page 160*

PUZZLE AND ILLUSTRATION BY PAUL RICHER

Triangle Tangle 3

Color in each area that has exactly three sides, and you'll see a scene from a place you might like to visit on a cold winter day.

Answer, page 160

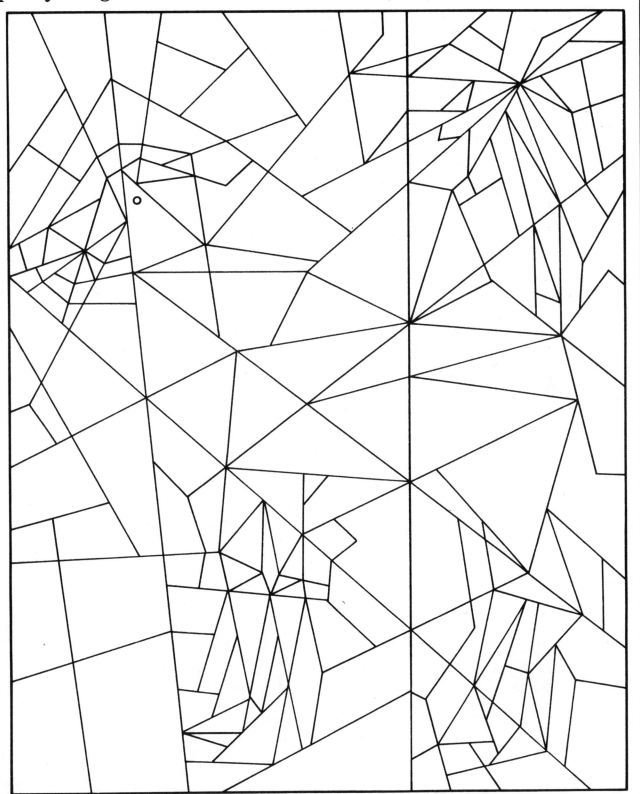

GAMES

Feet First

Our animal photographer needs to work on his aim. When we asked for pictures of 12 animals, this is what we got. Can you identify the animals from just their legs and feet?

Answers, page 161

1

2

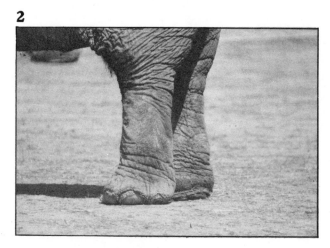

3

4

5

6

7

8

9

10

11

12

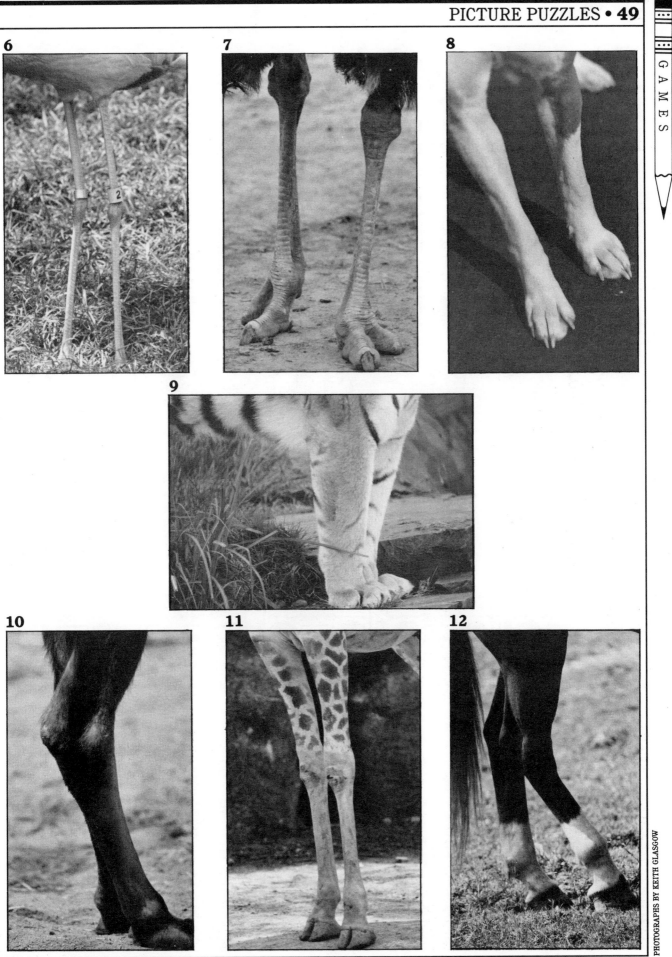

Assembly Line

In each row, three of the four products lettered A to D have errors that make them different from the correct model shown in the first column. Can you find the one perfect product in each row?

Answers, page 161

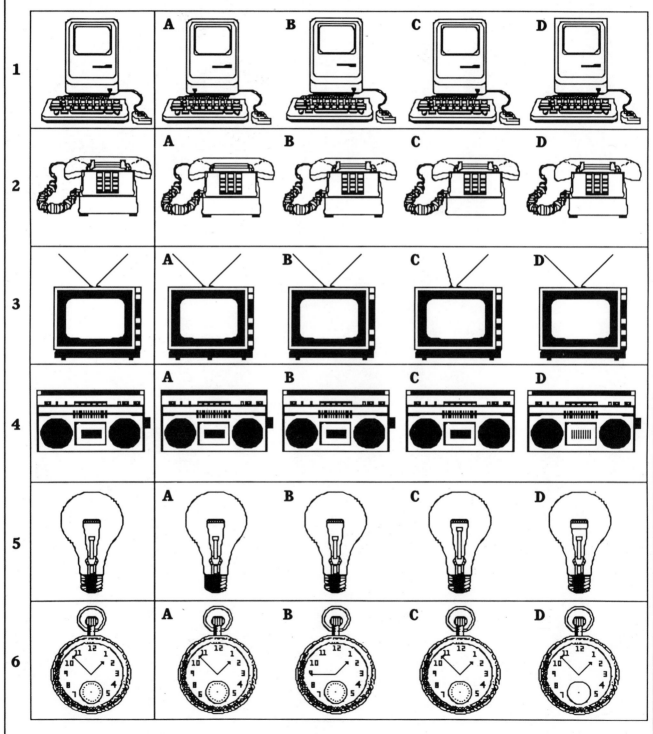

Ice Tease

Memory Test (Part One)

Junior and a couple of his friends decided to go ice skating. Study this ice rink scene for up to three minutes, then turn the page to test your memory.

PUZZLE BY KAREN ANDERSON/ILLUSTRATION BY ROLLIN MCGRAIL.

Ice Tease

Memory Test (Part Two)
(PLEASE DON'T READ THIS UNTIL YOU HAVE READ PAGE 51.)

How good is your memory? Consider yourself very attentive to detail if you can answer five of the seven questions correctly.

Answers, page 161

1. Junior was wearing a checkered jacket. Where was he?
2. How much time was left before the rink closed?
3. Were the skaters skating clockwise or counterclockwise?
4. What posted rule was one skater breaking?
5. Name two drinks being sold at the stand.
6. What symbol was on the jacket of the boy in the sunglasses?
7. Which one of these sports props was *not* in the scene?

Match-Up 4

These six snowmen look very similar, but only two are exactly alike. Can you find the two that match?

Answer, page 161

Secrets of the Swamp

Can you find the following things hidden in this swamp scene: book, boot, dart, feather, firecracker, flying duck, fork, ice cream cone, kite, paintbrush, pencil, pipe, scissors, sitting duck, sock, umbrella, whale? *Answers, page 161*

ILLUSTRATION BY MARK MAZUT

Strange Happenings

Have you ever seen a fruit bowl? If you have, it probably didn't look like the first picture below, showing a pear with a bowling ball. Instead, it probably looked like the fruit bowl on the bottom of the facing page.

Each of the illustrated activities (1–9) below is an unusual way of showing one of the objects (A–I) on the facing page. Can you match them up?

Answers, page 162

1

2

3

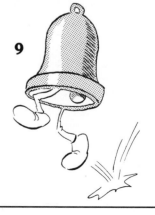

4

HIGHER WAGES!

5

NO, BUT SERIOUSLY, FOLKS!

6

7

8

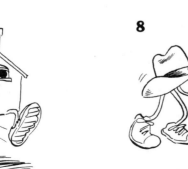

9

Whose Hues?

To complete this picture, color the areas according to the letters: R = red, Y = yellow, G = green, B = blue, P = purple, O = brown. *Answer, page 162*

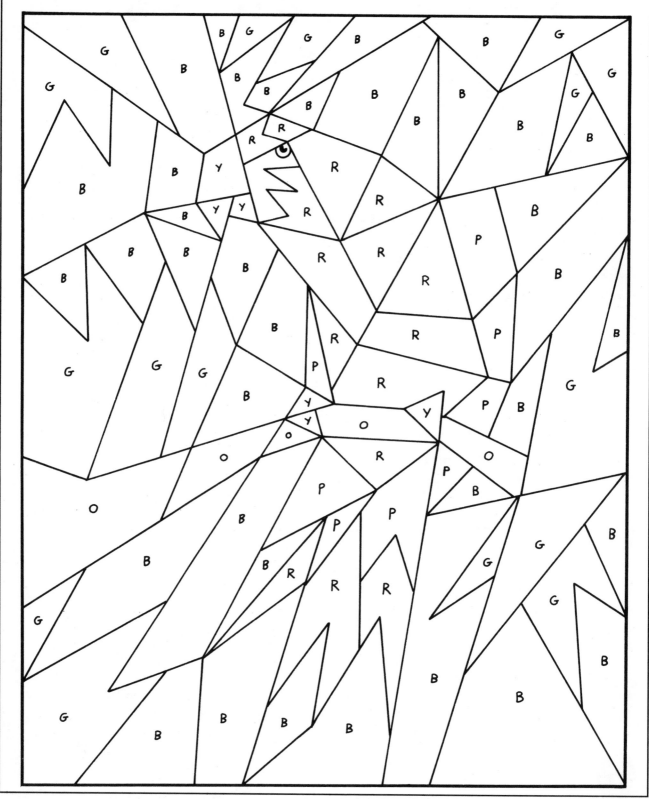

ILLUSTRATION BY MARK MAZUT

2

Word Play

Picture Crossword 1

To solve this crossword, enter the name of each object in its proper place in the grid.

Answers, page 162

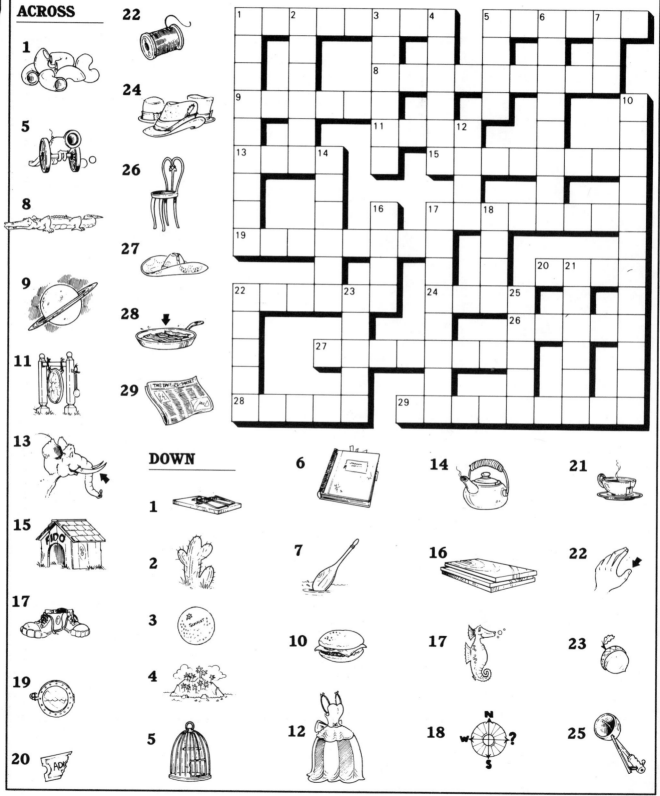

GAMES (vertical side tab)

ACROSS

1
5
8
9
11
13
15
17
19
20
22
24
26
27
28
29

DOWN

1
2
3
4
5
6
7
10
12
14
16
17
18
21
22
23
25

PUZZLE BY SCOTT MARLEY/ILLUSTRATION BY BOB ROSE

G A M E S

Pencil Pointers 1

In this crossword puzzle, the clues appear inside the grid. Fill in the answers in the direction of the arrows.

Answers, page 162

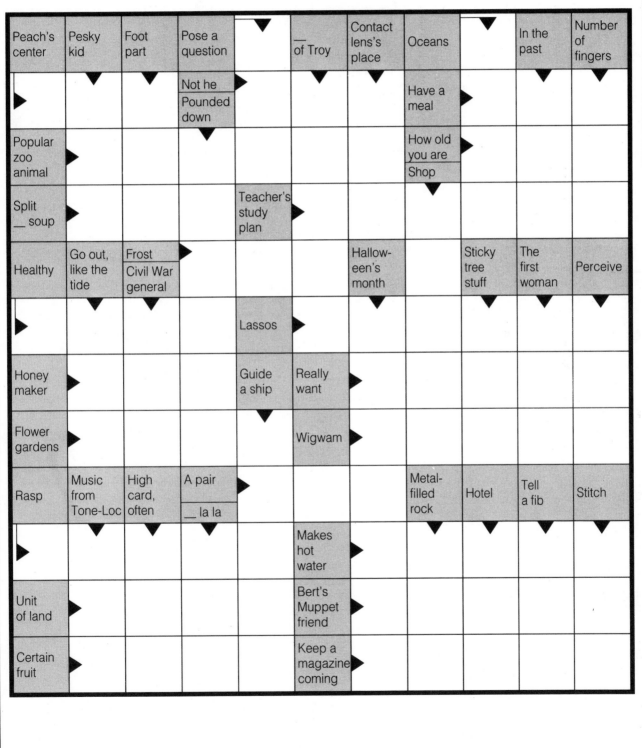

PUZZLE BY TRIP PAYNE

Spelling Beehive

How many words can you find in this honeycomb grid? You may start at any letter, then travel from space to space in any direction, spelling out a word as you go. You may use a space more than once in a word but you may not use the same letter twice in a row. For example, you could spell out SOLO by reusing the O, but you could not use the O twice in a row as in FOOL.

You can probably find many 3-letter and 4-letter words in the grid. But we've also found eleven 5-letter words, six 6-letter words, two 8-letter words, a 9-letter word, and a 10-letter word. If you can find 12 words of five letters or more, your eyes are as sharp as your vocabulary. *Answers, page 162*

Presidential Dessert

Unscramble the name of each United States president below and write it in the boxes following the letters. When you're finished, read down the shaded column to find the name of a dessert. *Answers, page 162*

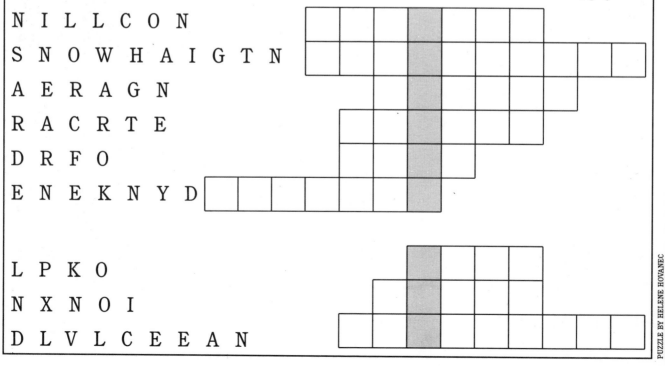

N I L L C O N

S N O W H A I G T N

A E R A G N

R A C R T E

D R F O

E N E K N Y D

L P K O

N X N O I

D L V L C E E A N

PUZZLE BY WAYNE SCHMITTBERGER

PUZZLE BY HELENE HOVANEC

Riddle Search 1

The names of the 22 musical instruments listed below are hidden in the grid of letters. Look across, back, down, up, and diagonally in the letters, and circle each instrument you discover. The word HORN has been circled as an example.

When you've circled all the instruments, write the *unused* letters from the grid on the blank spaces at the bottom of the page. Keep the letters in order, from left to right and from top to bottom, and you'll discover the answer to this riddle: WHY DID THE BOY PUT HIS HEAD ON THE PIANO?

Answers, page 162

```
B  U  G  L  E  B  G  M  A  B  U  T
K  A  Z  O  O  E  U  N  C  A  H  R
U  S  N  E  H  R  I  R  E  C  A  U
W  N  A  J  D  L  T  O  N  O  R  M
P  I  A  N  O  P  A  H  T  R  M  P
E  L  D  I  T  O  R  G  A  N  O  E
F  O  V  O  P  L  A  A  Y  E  N  T
L  D  F  I  F  E  R  E  H  T  I  Z
U  N  B  N  O  I  D  R  O  C  C  A
T  A  M  B  O  U  R  I  N  E  A  Y
E  M  O  L  O  C  C  I  P  E  A  R
```

ACCORDION
BANJO
BUGLE
CORNET
DRUM
FIFE
FLUTE

GUITAR
HARMONICA
HARP
HORN
KAZOO
MANDOLIN
OBOE
ORGAN

PIANO
PICCOLO
TAMBOURINE
TRUMPET
TUBA
VIOLIN
ZITHER

RIDDLE ANSWER: _ _ _ _ _ _ _ _ _ _ _ _ _

_ _ _ _ _ _ _ _ _ _ _ _ .

Disabled Vehicles

Parts of each of the 10 vehicles below have been removed, leaving them incomplete. Put each three-letter word from the right into one of the sets of empty spaces on the left to repair their names.

Answers, page 162

1.	A U T O _ _ _ I L E	ACT
2.	B _ _ _	AGO
3.	_ _ _ O E	CAN
4.	_ _ _ E D	HIP
5.	S _ _ _	MAR
6.	S U B _ _ _ I N E	MOB
7.	_ _ _ I	MOP
8.	T R _ _ _ O R	OAT
9.	T _ _ _	RAM
10.	W _ _ _ N	TAX

CAR Quiz

How many of these "CAR" words can you identify?
Put one letter on each blank.

Answers, page 162

1.	Ace or king, for example	C A R _
2.	Christmas song	C A R _ _
3.	Ship's freight	C A R _ _
4.	Transport	C A R _ _
5.	Food for a rabbit	C A R _ _ _
6.	Floor covering	C A R _ _ _
7.	Milk container	C A R _ _ _
8.	"Bugs Bunny," for one	C A R _ _ _ _
9.	Chewy candy	C A R _ _ _ _
10.	Traveling amusement show	C A R _ _ _ _ _
11.	Red bird	C A R _ _ _ _ _
12.	Worker with hammer and nails	C A R _ _ _ _ _ _

Crisscross Puzzle 1

The words below all rhyme with the word "eight." Place them into the diagram so that they interlock as in a crossword. When you are done, each word will have been used exactly once. One word has been filled in to start you off.

Answers, page 162

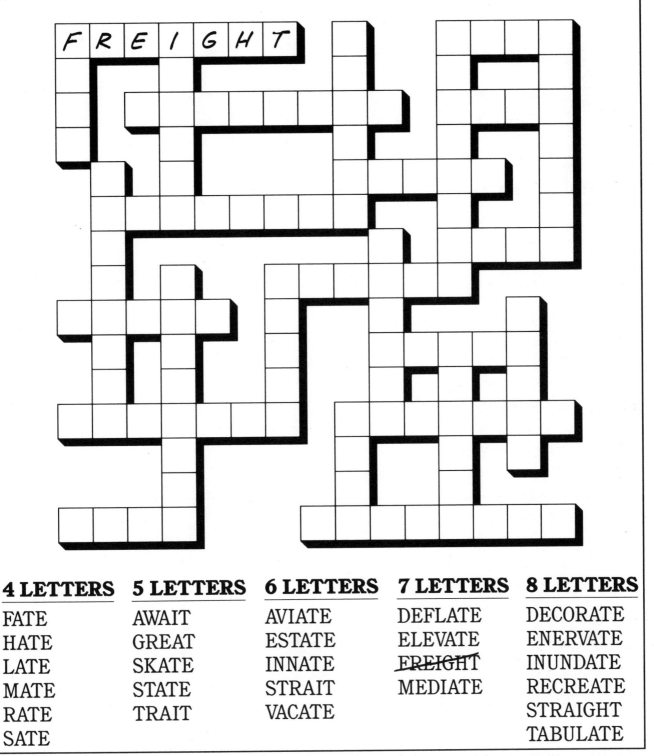

4 LETTERS	**5 LETTERS**	**6 LETTERS**	**7 LETTERS**	**8 LETTERS**
FATE	AWAIT	AVIATE	DEFLATE	DECORATE
HATE	GREAT	ESTATE	ELEVATE	ENERVATE
LATE	SKATE	INNATE	~~FREIGHT~~	INUNDATE
MATE	STATE	STRAIT	MEDIATE	RECREATE
RATE	TRAIT	VACATE		STRAIGHT
SATE				TABULATE

On the Double

Each object pictured on this page has the same name as one of the other objects shown. For example, there are two PITCHERS—the container and the baseball player. Can you match up the other picture pairs?

Answers, page 162

G A M E S

Crossword Puzzle 1

Answers, page 163

ACROSS

1 Drill part
4 Ugly rodent
7 No ifs, __, or buts
11 High card in poker
12 The last three sounds in "Old MacDonald Had a Farm"
13 Jewish book of scripture
15 Insect that might sting Bambi
17 Like very old bread
18 Nose-blowing paper
20 Diamond or ruby
21 Clothing tag
24 Mexican sandwich or salad
26 Ostrich-like bird
27 Where the moon rises
30 One-twelfth of a foot
33 New Jersey basketball team
35 Fib
36 Bushy hairstyle
37 Against: Prefix
38 Months when baseball season starts: Abbreviation
40 Once around the track
41 School test
43 Herb which is a homophone of TIME
45 Make a mistake
47 Yogi Bear's sidekick
50 Cartoon duck
52 Lightning bug
56 Farm buildings
57 President Eisenhower's nickname
58 Salmon eggs
59 Colors T-shirts
60 Koppel of ABC News
61 "__ a beautiful day in the neighborhood"

DOWN

1 Opposite of good
2 Cubes in the freezer
3 Golfer's prop
4 Do one's nails again
5 Is sick
6 Playthings
7 Out on a boat: 2 words
8 "To be or __ to be"
9 Long-winged mosquito-eating insect
10 Flea market event
14 Shorten pants
16 Rural __: Abbreviation
19 Say
21 Singer Horne
22 Prayer's ending
23 Colorful former caterpillar
25 U.S. spy organization: Abbreviation

28 Site of 1836 battle for Texas independence
29 Drink through a straw
31 Stuff (full)
32 Comedian Bob
34 Number of players on a volleyball team
39 Stashed food
42 Deep chasm
44 Gardening tool
45 Asner and Mister
46 Bug spray brand
48 Just for the fun __: 2 words
49 Ten-speed or tandem
51 Enemy
53 Last day of the school week: Abbreviation
54 Parking area
55 Word of agreement

PUZZLE BY KAREN ANDERSON

From House to House

In this maze you may travel one box at a time—up, down, left, or right, but *not* diagonally. Here's the catch: You may only move between boxes if the words in those boxes can be joined together, in order, to form a compound word. For example, you could move from a box with the word PAPER to a neighboring box with the word WEIGHT, since PAPERWEIGHT is a word. (You could not, however, move from WEIGHT to PAPER, since WEIGHTPAPER is not a word.)

Using these rules, can you find your way from the HOUSE in the upper left to the HOUSE in the lower right?

Answer, page 163

HOUSE	WORK	BOOK	WORM	SIDE	KICK	OFF	SET
FLY	PAPER	BACK	HOLE	WAY	WORK	HAND	BAG
LIFT	WEIGHT	GROUND	WATER	PARK	BRIDGE	SPRING	PIPE
OUT	WASH	HOG	SHED	BALL	FOOT	STEP	LINE
DOOR	HORSE	SAW	DUST	POINT	TENDER	SISTER	UP
STOP	OVER	SEE	PAN	HANDLE	BAR	COACH	STAGE
WATCH	OFF	SIDE	CAKE	WOOD	WIND	MAN	POWER
BAND	STAND	WALK	OUT	BOX	MILL	MAD	HOUSE

PUZZLE BY WAYNE SCHMITTBERGER

G A M E S

Fill-Ins 1

Complete each crossword grid with words that fit the given category.

Answers, page 163

FRUITS

FARM ANIMALS

WAYS TO TRAVEL

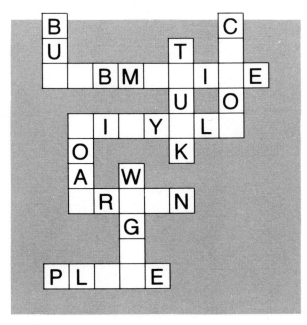

SPORTS

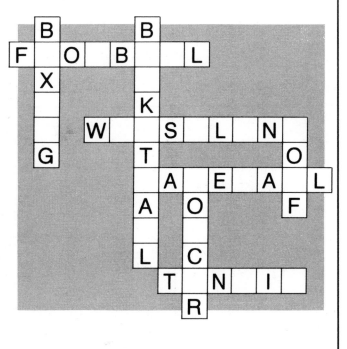

Collectors' Items

Each set of letters below is a scrambled name of a type of thing that some people collect. If you can unscramble the letters and write the answers in the boxes, the name of one more type of collection will appear in the shaded column. We've done the first one to get you started. *Answers, page 163*

1. ~~MICCO OBOK~~
2. PARAGHOUT
3. SPAMT
4. SELSELAH
5. TUTONB
6. COMOTHAKB
7. LDOL
8. TEBOLT PCA
9. NICO
10. QUINATE
11. RESPOT
12. REDROC

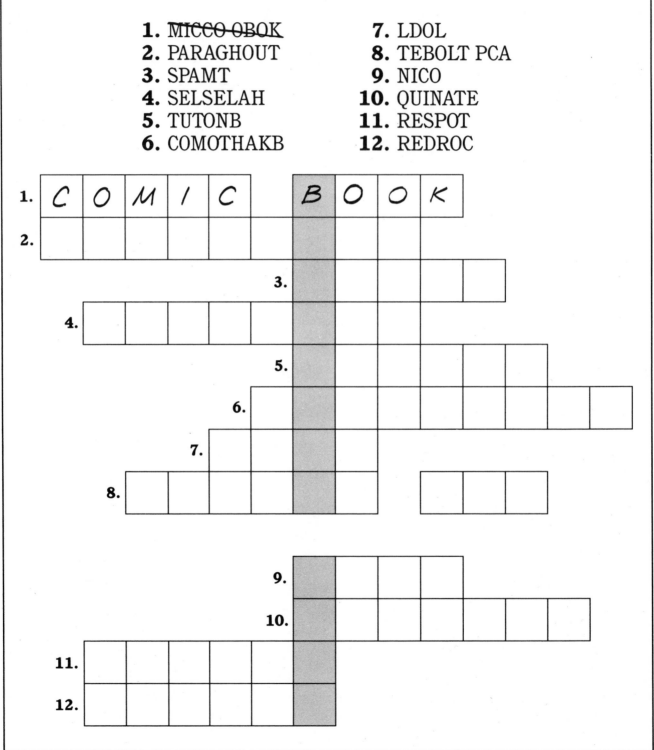

1. C O M I C | B O O K

Picture Crossword 2

To solve this crossword, enter the name of each object in its proper place in the grid.

Answers, page 163

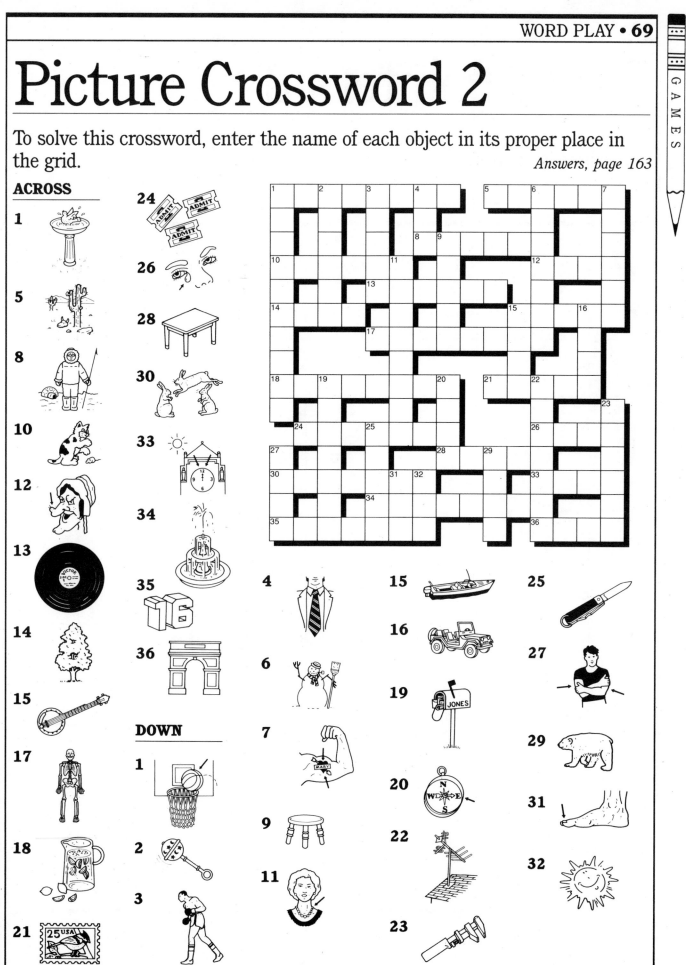

Pencil Pointers 2

In this crossword puzzle, the clues appear inside the grid. Fill in the answers in the direction of the arrows.

Answers, page 163

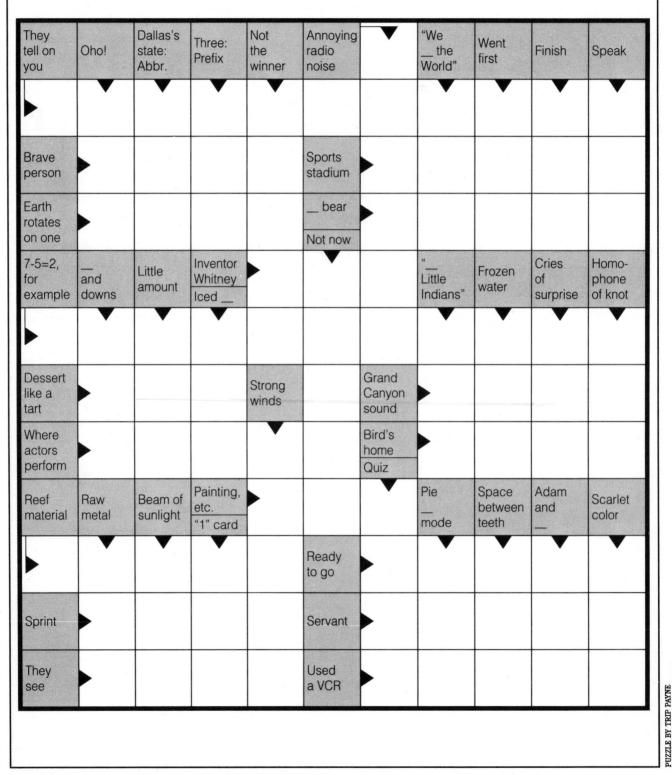

Sum Fun

First identify each picture. Then add and subtract the letters as indicated. If you do the puzzle correctly, the leftover letters will spell the name of somewhere interesting to go.   *Answer, page 163*

Presto-Chango

Change one letter in each word below to form a list of words that fit each heading. For example, the answer to A1, APPLY, is APPLE.   *Answers, page 163*

A. FRUITS
1. APPLY
2. DEMON
3. GRAPH
4. GRANGE
5. TANGO
6. CHEERY
7. FELON
8. LAME

B. FORMS OF TRANSPORTATION
1. GRAIN
2. BUM
3. PLANT
4. BULGY
5. BOOT
6. TRACK
7. BAR
8. FURRY

Pet Rebuses

First identify each picture. Then, spell out each word and add and subtract the letters as indicated. If you do the puzzles correctly, you will spell the names of five animals that make good pets.

Answers, page 164

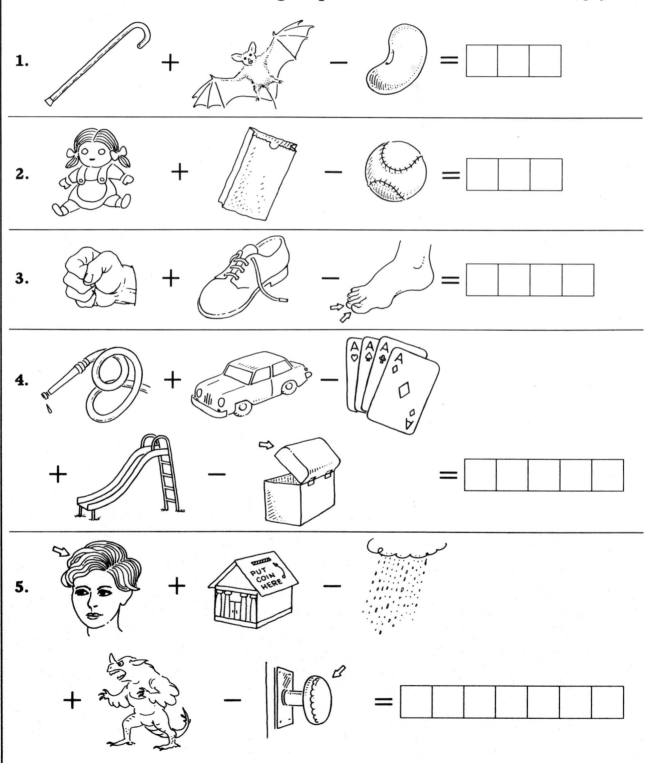

Crossword Puzzle 2

Answers, page 164

ACROSS

1 Hopping amphibian
5 Water surrounding a castle
9 Opposite of "on"
12 Cyclist's transportation
13 It connects a car's wheels
14 __ Grande (Texas river)
15 Not busy
16 It's the "First State"
18 Ski resort named for a tree
20 Bottoms of the feet
21 One or the __ (either)
23 That girl
24 Which person?
25 "__ upon a time ..."
28 Sign of an old wound
32 House light
34 Hearing organ
35 Dog in *The Wizard of Oz*
36 "Twinkle, twinkle, little __"
37 Region
39 Opposite of "high"
40 Rowboat part
42 Farmers harvest them
44 Opposite of "closes"
47 Javelin-like weapon
49 State called the "Old Dominion"
51 Job for a detective
54 Boxer Muhammad __
55 They complete small i's
56 Garden of __ (Adam and Eve setting)
57 Civil War general Robert E. __
58 Mothers of lambs
59 Highway

DOWN

1 Federal investigating group: Abbreviation
2 Get __ of (throw away)
3 It's the "Sooner State"
4 Birds that honk
5 Constructed
6 Cattle often in yokes
7 Everything
8 Make fun of
9 Spoken, as an exam
10 Flames
11 Enemies
17 Opposite of "best"
19 Player who gets paid
21 "Wise" birds
22 This and __
23 At this place
26 Close by
27 Automobile
29 It's the "Centennial State"
30 On the roof of
31 Lines, as of seats
33 Fork tine
38 High card in a deck
41 Toward the left or right
43 Auto used by an Indy 500 driver
44 Egg shape
45 Heap
46 One of the Great Lakes
47 Location
48 Throw the football
50 At this moment
52 The Mediterranean, for one
53 Finish

Riddle Search 2

The names of the 15 fruits listed below are hidden in the grid of letters. Look across, back, down, up, and diagonally in the letters, and circle each fruit you discover. The word PLUM has been circled as an example.

When you've circled all the fruits, write the *unused* letters from the grid on the blank spaces at the bottom of the page. Keep the letters in order, from left to right and from top to bottom, and you'll discover the answer to this riddle: WHY DON'T BANANAS EVER GET LONELY?

Answers, page 164

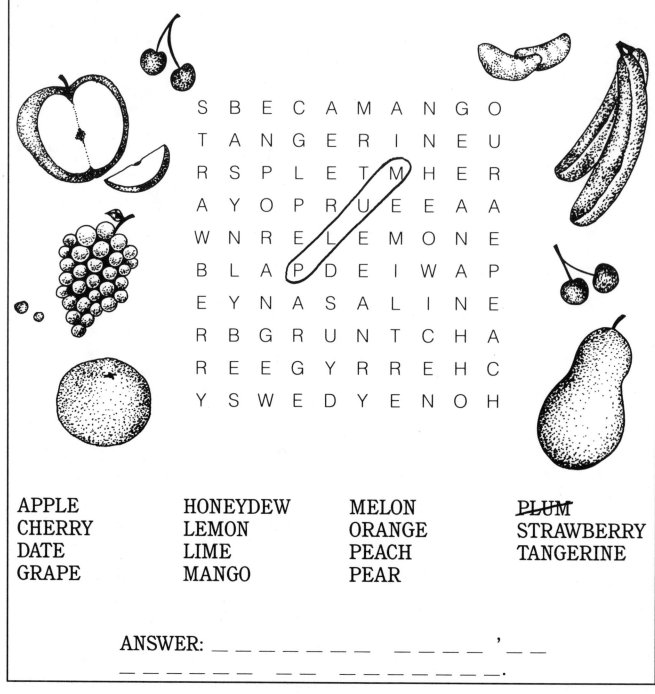

```
S  B  E  C  A  M  A  N  G  O
T  A  N  G  E  R  I  N  E  U
R  S  P  L  E  T  M  H  E  R
A  Y  O  P  R  U  E  E  A  A
W  N  R  E  L  E  M  O  N  E
B  L  A  P  D  E  I  W  A  P
E  Y  N  A  S  A  L  I  N  E
R  B  G  R  U  N  T  C  H  A
R  E  E  G  Y  R  R  E  H  C
Y  S  W  E  D  Y  E  N  O  H
```

APPLE	HONEYDEW	MELON	~~PLUM~~
CHERRY	LEMON	ORANGE	STRAWBERRY
DATE	LIME	PEACH	TANGERINE
GRAPE	MANGO	PEAR	

ANSWER: _ _ _ _ _ _ _ _ _ _ _ , _ _

_ _ _ _ _ _ _ _ _ _ _ _.

PUZZLE BY HELENE HOVANEC/ILLUSTRATIONS BY ROBERTA V. PRESSEL

Crisscross Puzzle 2

Place the mammal names below into the diagram so that they interlock as in a crossword. When you are done, each word will have been used exactly once. One word has been filled in to start you off.

Answers, page 164

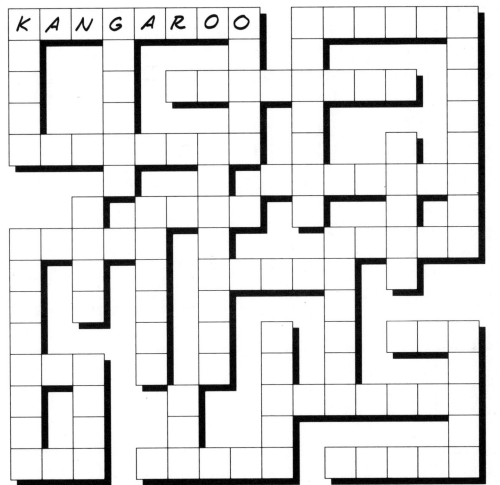

3 LETTERS

CAT
COW
DOG
RAT

4 LETTERS

DEER
GOAT
LION

5 LETTERS

CAMEL
CHIMP
HIPPO
HORSE
KOALA
OTTER
RHINO
STEER
TIGER
WHALE

6 LETTERS

COUGAR
DONKEY
GOPHER
WALRUS

7 LETTERS

GORILLA
PANTHER
WILDCAT

8 LETTERS

ANTEATER
ANTELOPE
ELEPHANT
KANGAROO
REINDEER
SQUIRREL

PUZZLE BY TRIP PAYNE

GAMES

Mirror Message

A palindrome is a word or phrase that is spelled the same backward and forward. An example is the sentence "MADAM, I'M ADAM." In a palindrome, punctuation and the spaces between words don't count— all that matters is the order of the letters.

Hidden in the grid below is a palindromic sentence. To find it, pretend that the heavy line through the middle of the grid is a mirror. Circle all the letters in the top half of the grid that are "reflected" in the correct places in the bottom half of the grid. (We've circled one to get you started.) Then read the circled letters from left to right and top to bottom, figure out where the spaces between words go, and you'll get some silly advice you might give someone named Otis.

Answers, page 164

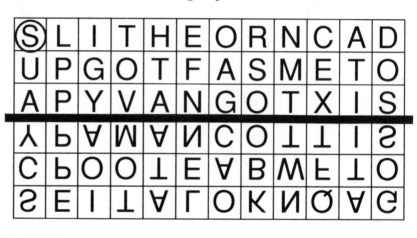

Mixed Pairs

Each missing word below has three letters. The two words in each sentence use the same letters rearranged to form different words. Can you fill in the blanks? *Answers, page 164*

Example: <u>NOW</u> that you came in first, you have <u>WON</u> the trophy.

1. I am _____ sure if an elephant weighs more than one _____.

2. _____ can you tell _____ is behind the Halloween mask?

3. The _____ is chasing the toy as an _____ for its master.

4. Rounding the bend, she drove the _____ in a wide _____.

5. The _____ holds enough water for a bath, _____ it leaks.

6. The cigar _____ _____ burned a hole in his coat.

7. Looking up, I _____ that he _____ in trouble.

8. _____ you sure that you have an _____ infection?

9. Were the people in town very _____ when the _____ overflowed?

PUZZLE BY WAYNE SCHMITTBERGER

PUZZLE BY GEORGE BREDEHORN

Now Hear This

In each column below, the letters of five words have been mixed up. When the letters are unscrambled, all five words in each column will rhyme. For example, OG and ETO in the first column unscramble to form GO and TOE. Can you solve the others?

Answers, page 164

1. **A.** OG   <u>GO</u>
   B. ETO   <u>TOE</u>
   C. OWM   _____
   D. WOLS _____
   E. GDOUH _____

2. **A.** EIL   _____
   B. GHHI _____
   C. YTR   _____
   D. UBY   _____
   E. EDY   _____

3. **A.** OOT   _____
   B. OHSE _____
   C. WREG _____
   D. ELBU _____
   E. RKNAAOGO _____

PUZZLE BY KAREN ANDERSON

Alphabetically Speaking

Place the words below into the boxes in alphabetical order, starting at the top. Then read down the fourth column to answer this riddle: WHERE SHOULD YOU PUT CRYING CHILDREN?

Answers, page 164

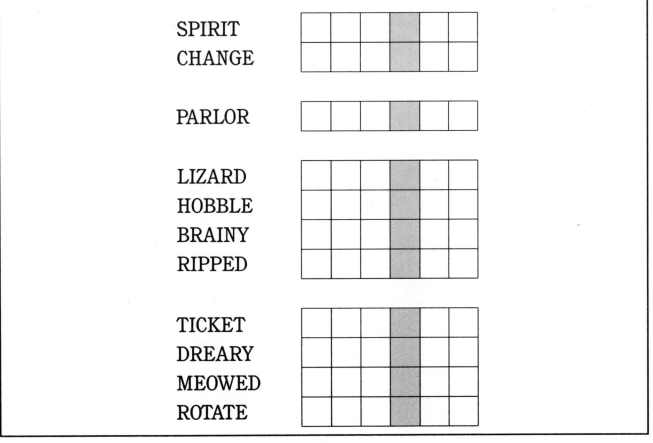

SPIRIT
CHANGE

PARLOR

LIZARD
HOBBLE
BRAINY
RIPPED

TICKET
DREARY
MEOWED
ROTATE

PUZZLE BY HELENE HOVANEC

Crossword Puzzle 3

Answers, page 164

ACROSS

1 Commercials
4 Cake found by the tub
8 North ___ (Santa's home)
12 What partygoers dunk chips into
13 Parrot's enclosure
14 Opposite of "shut"
15 Cartoon artist
17 Unwanted plant in the garden
18 Iron or copper
19 ___-friendly (like well-written computer programs)
21 Disorderly state
24 Snares
27 Bug that bugs beagles
30 ___ fish salad
32 Make a knot
33 Petroleum product
34 Water ___ (steam)
35 Half of two
36 She lived in 58-Across
37 Where your pupils are
38 ___ and crafts
39 Number of Dwarfs
41 Fishing rod part
43 Insects that make hills
45 Grown-up person
49 Dislike strongly
51 Copycat
54 Tiny chemical particle
55 Spotted cubes used in games
56 Pretty ___ picture: 2 words
57 "Quite contrary" girl
58 Genesis garden
59 Homophone of "hay"

DOWN

1 He lived with 36-Across
2 Have a meal
3 Get rid of watermelon seeds, in a way
4 Weighing device
5 Cereal grain
6 Long ___ (years in the past)
7 Its capital is Lima
8 Physical might
9 Telephone company worker
10 ___ Majors (actor)
11 Conclusion
16 Papa Bear's wife
20 Five pointed figure
22 Remain
23 Great, like Clark Kent
25 Half a quart
26 Looks at
27 Opponents
28 "As I ___ and breathe"
29 It can take you to the top floor
31 You smell with it
34 Opening to let air out
38 Actor Alan from TV's *M*A*S*H*
40 Opponent
42 Consumed
44 ___ view (profile)
46 Salt Lake City's State
47 Take last place
48 Waiter's carrying aid
49 Meat from a pig
50 One day ___ time: 2 words
52 Prefix meaning "center"
53 Frozen water

Body Building

Each item illustrated on this page shares its name with a part of the human body. Can you write each item's number in the matching body area? We've done the first one, FOOT, to get you started.

Answers, page 165

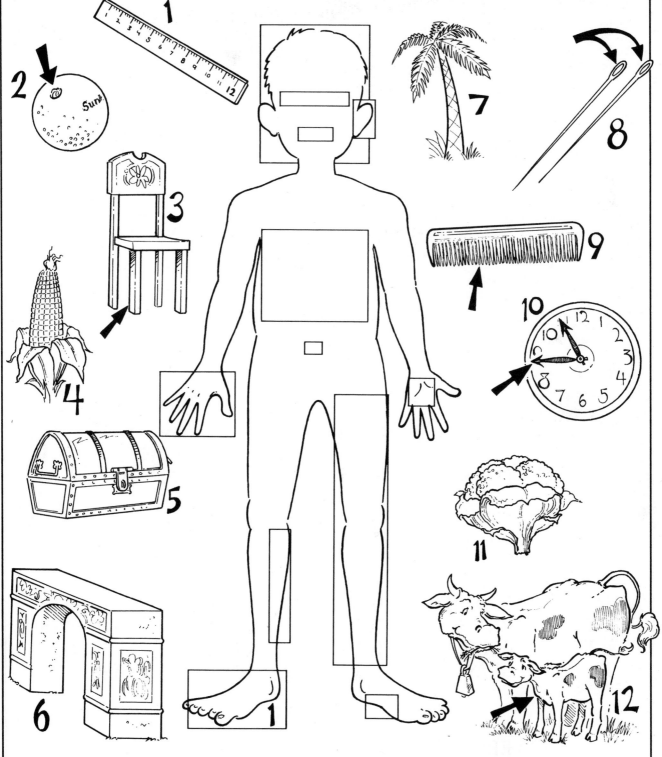

Riddle Search 3

The names of the 21 colors listed below are hidden in the grid of letters. Look across, back, down, up, and diagonally in the letters, and circle each color you discover. The word AQUA has been circled as an example.

When you've circled all the colors, write the *unused* letters from the grid on the blank spaces at the bottom of the page. Keep the letters in order, from left to right and from top to bottom, and you'll discover the answer to this riddle: WHAT IS BLACK AND WHITE AND RED ALL OVER? *Answers, page 165*

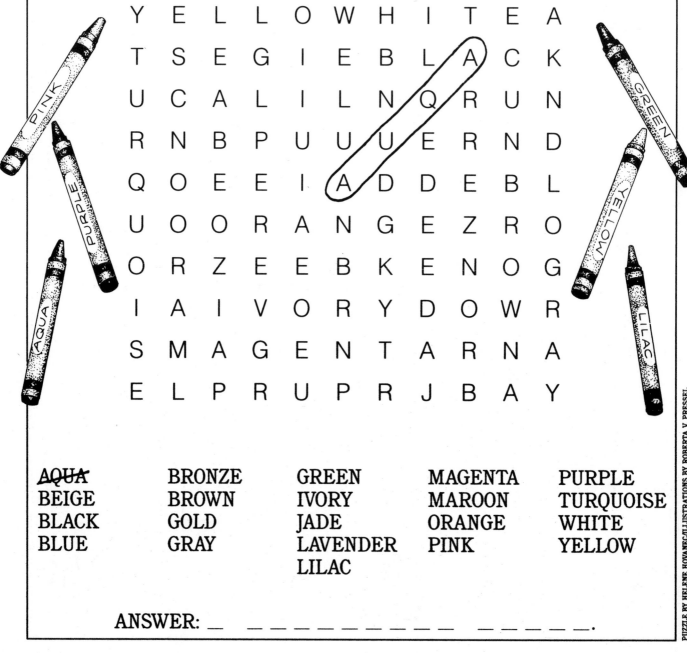

```
Y  E  L  L  O  W  H  I  T  E  A
T  S  E  G  I  E  B  L  A  C  K
U  C  A  L  I  L  N  Q  R  U  N
R  N  B  P  U  U  U  E  R  N  D
Q  O  E  E  I  A  D  D  E  B  L
U  O  O  R  A  N  G  E  Z  R  O
O  R  Z  E  E  B  K  E  N  O  G
I  A  I  V  O  R  Y  D  O  W  R
S  M  A  G  E  N  T  A  R  N  A
E  L  P  R  U  P  R  J  B  A  Y
```

AQUA	BRONZE	GREEN	MAGENTA	PURPLE
BEIGE	BROWN	IVORY	MAROON	TURQUOISE
BLACK	GOLD	JADE	ORANGE	WHITE
BLUE	GRAY	LAVENDER	PINK	YELLOW
		LILAC		

ANSWER: __ _____ _____.

PUZZLE BY HELENE HOVANEC/ILLUSTRATIONS BY ROBERTA V. PRESSEL

GAMES

Picture Crossword 3

To solve this crossword, enter the name of each object in its proper place in the grid.

Answers, page 165

ACROSS

DOWN

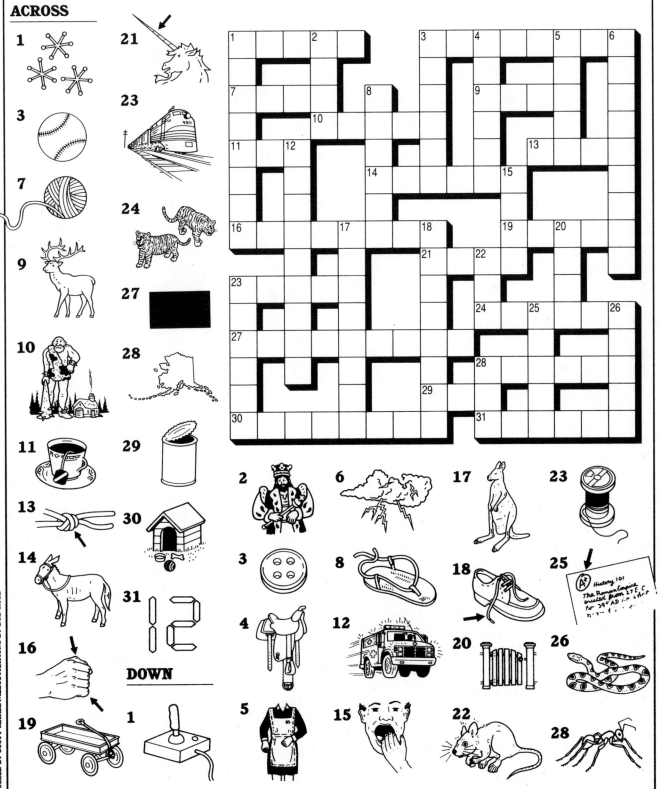

Crossword Puzzle 4

ACROSS

Answers, page 165

1 Cleverness
4 __ and tell
8 Smack with an open hand
12 Commotion
13 Manufactured
14 Love's opposite
15 Dog doc
16 Last word of a prayer
17 Ajar, as a door
18 Painter's stand
20 Traffic sign with eight sides
22 TV alien from Melmac
24 Employing
28 Burn to a crisp
31 Where the sun rises
34 Look at
35 Falling balls of ice and snow
36 Museum exhibits
37 Close the door with force
38 Ancient
39 __ code (long distance prefix)
40 Partner of "his"
41 Modeled
43 Sticky stuff or a baby talk syllable
45 Look at words in a book
48 Pester or make fun of
52 Tale
55 Money
57 __ and downs
58 Gets older
59 Birch or walnut
60 Mr. Van Winkle
61 Music symbol
62 Alpha Centauri or the sun
63 "Have you __ wool?"

DOWN

1 "Goodbye" gesture
2 Thought
3 Young children
4 Tiny
5 Seuss's *Green Eggs and* __
6 Poetry
7 "This little piggy __ to market..."
8 Buys groceries
9 Once around the track
10 Dined
11 Ball-point or felt-tip
19 English title
21 Gone for lunch
23 Phobia
25 Small piece of land surrounded by water
26 Close by
27 Jewels
28 Cut of lamb or pork
29 Angel's "hat"
30 Helps
32 "You __ So Beautiful..."
33 Male deer
37 Footwear
39 Summer drink
42 Rub out with a pencil end
44 In __ words (stated differently)
46 Performs
47 Small target arrow
49 Distinctive atmosphere
50 Twirl
51 Catch sight of
52 __ Francisco, California
53 In the past
54 Receive
56 Mediterranean or Black

G A M E S

Word Wheel

Fill each of the 16 spaces of the wheel with a three-letter word that is the same as the word on each side of it except for one letter. (Like PIG, PEG, LEG, LOG, etc.) Start with the given word FIX and continue around the wheel. Each answer word is pictured (in no particular order) somewhere on this page.

Answers, page 165

FIX

PAN Handling

Don't PANic—we just want to see how many of these "PAN" words you can identify. Put one letter on each blank.

Answers, page 165

1. Window glass   P A N _
2. Piece of wood   P A N _ _
3. Flower   P A N _ _
4. Chinese bear-like animal   P A N _ _
5. Trousers   P A N _ _
6. Country with a canal   P A N _ _ _
7. Food closet   P A N _ _ _
8. Black leopard   P A N _ _ _ _
9. Flapjack   P A N _ _ _ _
10. Body part that helps digestion   P A N _ _ _ _ _
11. Gesture without speech   P A N _ _ _ _ _ _
12. Total chaos   P A N _ _ _ _ _ _ _

Here Hear!

Homophones are words that sound alike, but are spelled differently and have different meanings. WON and ONE are homophones, and so are TWO and TO (and TOO, too!). Can you complete the sentences below by filling in each pair of blanks with a pair of homophones?

Answers, page 165

1. Luckily, the window was open when I accidentally _____ the ball _____ it.

2. The carpenter _____ a hole through the _____.

3. After _____ the cracks in the _____, I was ready to paint.

4. The hotel _____ correctly _____ the way to the pool.

5. Never before had such a _____ been _____.

Riddle Search 4

The names of the 19 kinds of dances listed below are hidden in the grid of letters. Look across, back, down, up, and diagonally in the letters, and circle each dance you discover. The word BOLERO has been circled as an example.

When you've circled all the dances, write the *unused* letters from the grid on the blank spaces at the bottom of the page. Keep the letters in order, from left to right and from top to bottom, and you'll find the answer to this riddle: WHAT DANCE DID THE PILGRIMS DO? *Answers, page 165*

```
H  O  K  E  Y  P  O  K  E  Y
T  U  H  E  T  E  U  N  I  M
P  O  L  K  A  P  L  Y  W  O
O  C  H  A  C  H  A  A  Y  N
H  J  I  G  H  M  L  O  D  K
Y  T  W  O  S  T  E  P  N  E
N  U  R  L  Z  T  W  H  I  Y
N  A  E  C  O  B  M  I  L  R
U  O  E  C  A  B  M  A  S  K
B  O  L  E  R  O  G  N  A  T
```

BOLERO	HORA	MINUET	TANGO
BUNNY HOP	HULA	MONKEY	TWIST
CHA-CHA	JIG	POLKA	TWO-STEP
CLOG	LIMBO	REEL	WALTZ
HOKEY-POKEY	LINDY	SAMBA	

RIDDLE ANSWER: _ _ _ _   _ _ _ _ _ _ _ _ _ .

PUZZLE BY HELENE HOVANEC

GAMES

Riddle Acrostic

Answer each clue and write the word on the numbered blanks. Then put each letter into the diagram in the matching numbered square. Work back and forth between the clues and the diagram to fill all the spaces. When you're finished, read the grid from left to right, starting at the top, and you'll find a riddle and its answer.

Answers, page 165

1	2	3	4	■	5	6	7	■	8	9
10	■	11	12	13	14	15	16	■	17	18
19	20	21	■	22	23	24	■	25	26	■
27	28	29	■	30	31	32	33	34	?	■
35	36	37	38	39	40	■	41	42	43	44
■	45	46	47	48	49	■	50	51	52	53

CLUES

A. Small
___ ___ ___ ___ ___ ___
33 6 4 8 52 15

B. Male parent
___ ___ ___ ___ ___ ___
35 3 25 46 28 44

C. Not soft
___ ___ ___ ___
2 23 16 5

D. Very sloppy
___ ___ ___ ___ ___
11 51 22 37 41

E. 4 + 4 =
___ ___ ___ ___ ___
39 32 17 27 49

F. Little Red Riding ___
___ ___ ___ ___
14 19 42 7

G. Very warm
___ ___ ___
31 12 38

H. Opposite of worst
___ ___ ___ ___
50 47 20 13

I. It's worn on the wrist
___ ___ ___ ___ ___
1 36 53 30 9

J. A place where a family might live
___ ___ ___ ___ ___
18 26 43 45 10

K. Not wet
___ ___ ___
34 29 24

L. Number of "Little Indians"
___ ___ ___
21 48 40

PUZZLE BY HELENE HOVANEC

Crisscross Puzzle 3

Place the U.S. cities below into the diagram so that they interlock as in a crossword. When you are done, each city will have been used exactly once.

Answers, page 165

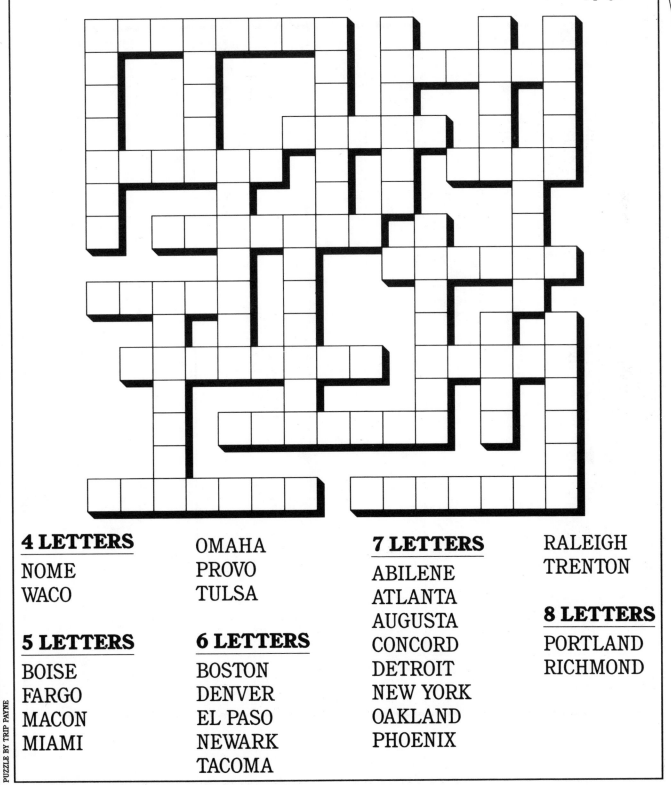

4 LETTERS
NOME
WACO

5 LETTERS
BOISE
FARGO
MACON
MIAMI

OMAHA
PROVO
TULSA

6 LETTERS
BOSTON
DENVER
EL PASO
NEWARK
TACOMA

7 LETTERS
ABILENE
ATLANTA
AUGUSTA
CONCORD
DETROIT
NEW YORK
OAKLAND
PHOENIX

RALEIGH
TRENTON

8 LETTERS
PORTLAND
RICHMOND

PUZZLE BY TRIP PAYNE

Pencil Pointers 3

In this crossword puzzle, the clues appear inside the grid. Fill in the answers in the direction of the arrows.

Answers, page 166

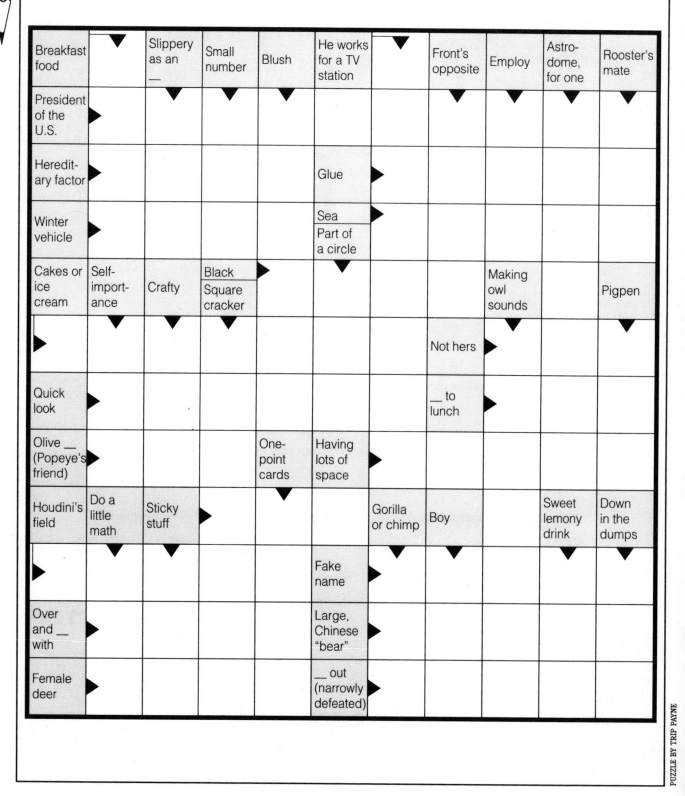

PUZZLE BY TRIP PAYNE

Among the Flowers

The answers to the 17 clues below are hidden in the flower names at the end of each line. To find them, cross off some of the letters in each flower's name; the remaining letters will spell the answer, reading from left to right. Budding puzzle solvers should be able to answer at least 10.

Answers, page 166

Example: Opposite of faster   *SLOWER*   SU̶N̶FLOWER

1. Twenty-four hours   _____ DAISY
2. Animal doctor   _____ VIOLET
3. 5,280 feet   _____ MISTLETOE
4. Wise bird   _____ COWSLIP
5. House servant   _____ MARIGOLD
6. Small breed of horse _____ PEONY
7. Spring month   _____ AMARYLLIS
8. Snake sound   _____ HIBISCUS
9. Male cow   _____ BLUEBELL
10. Hair parter   _____ COLUMBINE
11. More aged   _____ GOLDENROD
12. Suggest   _____ HYACINTH
13. Sneak around   _____ SNOWDROP
14. Half a quart   _____ POINSETTIA
15. Egg holder   _____ CARNATION
16. Cook's wear   _____ SNAPDRAGON
17. National song   _____ CHRYSANTHEMUM

Riddle Search 5

The names of the 20 green things listed below are hidden in the grid of letters. Look across, back, down, up, and diagonally in the letters, and circle each green thing you discover. The word CELERY has been circled as an example.

    When you've circled all the green things, write the *unused* letters from the grid on the blank spaces at the bottom of the page. Keep the letters in order, from left to right and from top to bottom, and you'll discover the answer to this riddle: WHAT IS GREEN AND SINGS? *Answers, page 166*

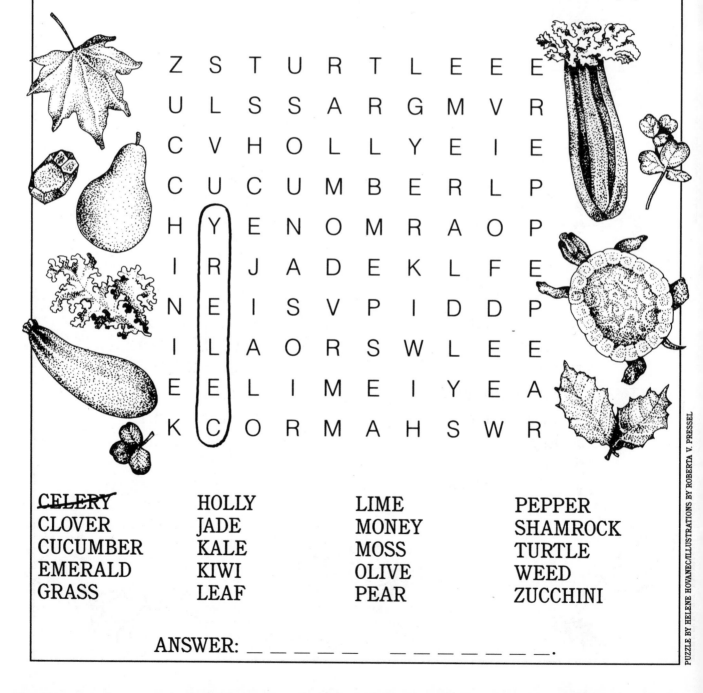

```
Z  S  T  U  R  T  L  E  E  E
U  L  S  S  A  R  G  M  V  R
C  V  H  O  L  L  Y  E  I  E
C  U  C  U  M  B  E  R  L  P
H  Y  E  N  O  M  R  A  O  P
I  R  J  A  D  E  K  L  F  E
N  E  I  S  V  P  I  D  D  P
I  L  A  O  R  S  W  L  E  E
E  E  L  I  M  E  I  Y  E  A
K  C  O  R  M  A  H  S  W  R
```

~~CELERY~~	HOLLY	LIME	PEPPER
CLOVER	JADE	MONEY	SHAMROCK
CUCUMBER	KALE	MOSS	TURTLE
EMERALD	KIWI	OLIVE	WEED
GRASS	LEAF	PEAR	ZUCCHINI

ANSWER: _ _ _ _ _ _   _ _ _ _ _ _ _ _.

PUZZLE BY HELENE HOVANEC/ILLUSTRATIONS BY ROBERTA V. PRESSEL

PuZZling Fill-Ins

How many of these "double Z" words can you identify? Put one letter on each blank. *Answers, page 166*

1. Bumble bee's sound   _ _ Z Z
2. Soda pop bubbles   _ _ Z Z
3. Type of music   _ _ Z Z
4. Pie topped with tomato sauce and cheese   _ _ Z Z _
5. How you'll feel if you spin around too fast   _ _ Z Z _
6. Soft, like a teddy bear   _ _ Z Z _
7. Curly hair, sometimes   _ _ _ Z Z _
8. Part of a gas pump   _ _ Z Z _ _
9. Sound made by frying bacon   _ _ Z Z _ _
10. Device to keep a dog from biting   _ _ Z Z _ _
11. Vulture-like bird   _ _ Z Z _ _ _
12. Light rain   _ _ _ Z Z _ _
13. Stick used to stir drinks   _ _ _ Z Z _ _
14. Big bear   _ _ _ Z Z _ _
15. Severe snowstorm   _ _ _ Z Z _ _ _

Bumper Crop

In each pair of words below, the second word contains all but one of the letters in the first word. Write the missing letter in the box between the words. When you're done, read down the columns to find the name of something related to the first words of each pair. *Answers, page 166*

LEAF		ALE		HEDGE		HEED
PETAL		TAPE		ASTER		REST
HOSE		SHE		ROOT		TOO
WATER		TEAR		ORCHID		CHOIR
WEED		DEW		MAPLE		LAMP
SHRUB		BUSH		LAWN		AWL

PUZZLE BY ANDREA CARLA MICHAELS

PUZZLE BY HELENE HOVANEC

G A M E S

Build-a-Word

Listed below are two sets of three-letter words. Each word in Column A can be combined with some word in Column B, with the Column A word coming first, to form a new word. One beginning may match more than one ending, but only one combination will use every word. We've done one to get you started.

Answers, page 166

A	**B**	
~~PAN~~	DEW	*PANTRY*
PEP	HER	_____
GOT	ICE	_____
CAR	PER	_____
MIL	RED	_____
NOT	ROT	_____
SAC	TEN	_____
CAN	TON	_____
RAT	~~TRY~~	_____
COT	YON	_____

PUZZLE BY ANDREA CARLA MICHAELS

Horsing Around

Each of the answers to the 7 clues below is the name of a well-known horse. Answer each clue, putting one letter per box. When you're finished, read down the shaded column of boxes to find the name of a bonus horse.

Answers, page 166

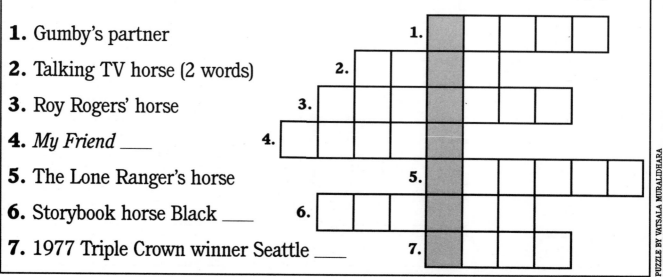

1. Gumby's partner

2. Talking TV horse (2 words)

3. Roy Rogers' horse

4. *My Friend* ___

5. The Lone Ranger's horse

6. Storybook horse Black ___

7. 1977 Triple Crown winner Seattle ___

PUZZLE BY VATSALA MURALIDHARA

Crossword Puzzle 5

Answers, page 166

ACROSS

1 Shoot with a ray gun
4 Place for a barn
8 Comedian's wisecrack
12 Metal source
13 Bassoon's relative
14 Inspires with respect
15 Tennis court divider
16 Gas used in advertising lights
17 They write in ink
18 Lessened, like pain or tension
20 Large brass instrument
22 Sweet potato
24 Beneath
28 Walk in shallow water
31 They change on birthdays
34 "Roses __ red . . ."
35 Colors
36 Money paid to the government
37 Middle East country whose capital is Tehran
38 Had some food
39 Sandwich shop
40 Relax
41 Part of the body from the waist to the neck
43 Coffee's alternative
45 Opposite of more
48 Group of soldiers or policemen
52 Container
55 Sets of first aid tools
57 __ as a fox
58 Muscle pain
59 What a light bulb means in cartoons
60 She lived in Eden
61 Honk
62 Opposite of admit
63 Mom's husband

DOWN

1 End __ (end of a football field)
2 Region
3 Dogs, cats, and fish
4 Actress Jane
5 Lincoln's nickname
6 Part of a plant that is below the ground
7 List of food choices at a restaurant
8 Country famous for electronics
9 Be in debt
10 Barbie's boyfriend
11 The 19th letter of the alphabet
19 What you see with
21 Yellow school vehicle
23 Companion
25 Make a challenge
26 Periods of time
27 What a tenant pays
28 Questioning word
29 Car
30 They play with the antelope, in song
32 Female version of "guy"
33 Way out of a room
37 Middle East country whose capital is Baghdad
39 A female 30-Down
42 Take a long nap
44 School paper that is often 500-words long
46 Slide on an icy road
47 Not the front or the back
49 __-car salesman
50 Thomas Edison's middle name
51 Colored, as Easter eggs
52 Taxi
53 Playing card with one pip
54 That girl
56 Seven plus three

Proverbial Confusion

Proverbs are supposed to offer good advice. But sometimes, different proverbs seem to say opposite things. We've taken three pairs of contradictory proverbs, and mixed up the order of the words in each proverb. Can you unscramble them?

Answers, page 166

Pair #1
NEVER TOO TO LEARN IT'S LATE.
NEW DOG CAN'T TEACH AN OLD TRICKS YOU.

Pair #2
SHALL FIND AND SEEK YOU.
THE CAT KILLED CURIOSITY.

Pair #3
ONE TWO ARE BETTER THAN HEADS.
THE BROTH COOKS SPOIL TOO MANY.

Fill-Ins 2

How many of these 12 words starting with "BAR" can you identify? Put one letter on each blank.

Answers, page 166

1. Dog sound   B A R _
2. Farm building   B A R _
3. Flat-bottomed boat   B A R _ _
4. Haircutter   B A R _ _ _
5. Cereal grain   B A R _ _ _
6. Wooden container   B A R _ _ _
7. Fashionable doll   B A R _ _ _
8. Fence or obstruction   B A R _ _ _ _
9. A good deal, at a flea market B A R _ _ _ _
10. Hair clasp   B A R _ _ _ _ _
11. Fish with sharp teeth B A R _ _ _ _ _
12. Air pressure gauge   B A R _ _ _ _ _ _

PUZZLE BY ANDREA CARLA MICHAELS

Riddlegrams

To solve a Riddlegram, fill in the answers to the clues, one letter on each blank. Then transfer the letters to the boxes above that have the same numbers. When all the boxes are filled in correctly, you will have the answer to a riddle.

Answers, page 166

RIDDLE #1: What wears a glass slipper and goes up and down tall buildings?

1	2	3	4	5	6	7	8	9	10	11	12	13	14

A. $\overline{}_{8}\ \overline{}_{2}\ \overline{}_{3}\ \overline{}_{7}$ Something you "wait in" at the store

B. $\overline{}_{4}\ \overline{}_{5}\ \overline{}_{9}\ \overline{}_{6}$ The kind of animal Bambi is

C. $\overline{}_{10}\ \overline{}_{13}\ \overline{}_{12}\ \overline{}_{5}$ What citizens do to elect the president

D. $\overline{}_{1}\ \overline{}_{11}\ \overline{}_{14}\ \overline{}_{4}$ Jack, queen, king, or ace

RIDDLE #2: What is purple, lies in the ocean, and is ruled by a queen?

1	2	3	4	5

6	7	8	9	10	11	12

A. $\overline{}_{6}\ \overline{}_{3}\ \overline{}_{1}$ Something to carry groceries in

B. $\overline{}_{9}\ \overline{}_{2}\ \overline{}_{10}\ \overline{}_{11}\ \overline{}_{12}$ Locomotive

C. $\overline{}_{7}\ \overline{}_{8}\ \overline{}_{4}$ Tear in two

D. $\overline{}_{12}\ \overline{}_{5}\ \overline{}_{3}\ \overline{}_{2}$ Not far

Seeing Things

Each of the illustrations below is a lighthearted, literal drawing of the name of a common thing. For instance, a star firing a squirt gun would be a SHOOTING STAR. How many of the words below can you identify? *Answers, page 166*

1

2

3

4

5

6

7

8

3

Games
& Trivia

Dinosaur Quiz

Dinosaurs were remarkable creatures that ruled the earth for millions of years. Much is still debated about them, such as the cause of their extinction and whether or not they were warm-blooded. Luckily, enough is known to write a quiz. We don't expect you to know all of the answers to these questions, but we do expect you'll find some interesting facts here.

Answers, page 166

1. The word "dinosaur" means
   a. terrible lizard
   b. angry giant
   c. living mountain
   d. make-believe monster

2. The dinosaurs lived mainly in a geologic time called the Mesozoic period, which began 245 million years ago and ended 66 million years ago. If you draw a timeline chart in which 1,000 years equals one inch (so that the time of Christ and Julius Caesar is two inches away), the dinosaurs will be approximately how far away?
   a. 500 to 750 feet
   b. 1,000 to 2,000 feet
   c. 1 to 2 miles
   d. 5 to 6 miles

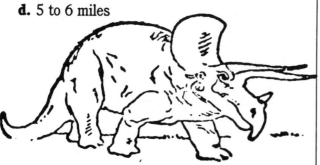

3. The anklyosaur had a unique defense against predators. It would
   a. use its trumpet-like horn to alert all nearby anklyosaurs to come and help.
   b. put out spikes that were normally retracted into its ankles and use these to ward off the predator.
   c. crouch down so that only its armored back was exposed and use its club-like tail to beat off its foes.
   d. hold up a mirror so that the other dinosaur, seeing how ugly it was, would run off to the nearest beauty parlor.

4. A tyrannosaur would often eat a stegosaur. True or False?

5. There was a species of dinosaur with two heads. True or False?

6. The brain of a stegosaur was twice the size of a human brain. True or False?

7. Despite its size and reputation, the tyrannosaur's stride was only about three feet. True or False?

8. Which one of these kinds of dinosaurs is a fake?
   a. Hadrosaurus A duck-billed dinosaur, it had 2,000 teeth in its mouth. When eating plants, it would grind down old teeth at a voracious rate and replace them with new ones.
   b. Phobosaurus A crocodile-like dinosaur, its skull was six feet long. It was one of the largest dinosaurs ever, measuring up to 50 feet in length.
   c. Spinosaurus A dinosaur with a "sail," this beast may have circulated blood through the large, fleshy fan on its back to cool itself.
   d. Borosaurus A plant-eating dinosaur with a drill on its tail, this animal could dig holes very quickly in order to escape its predators.

WRITTEN BY KAREN ANDERSON

G A M E S

Dinosaur Eyeball Benders

Below are close-up drawings of eight prehistoric creatures. Some are
dinosaurs and some are not. Can you identify the creatures, and tell which are
not true dinosaurs?

Answers, page 167

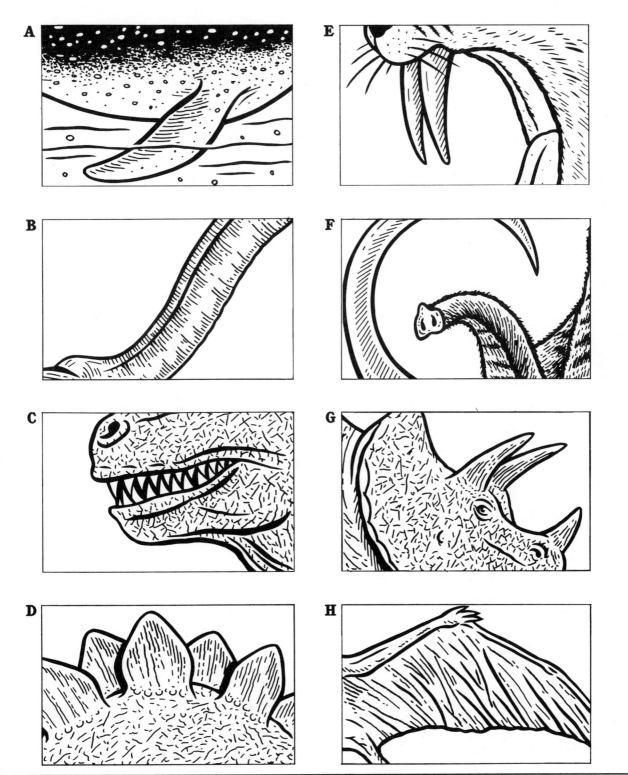

A

B

C

D

E

F

G

H

ILLUSTRATIONS BY MARK MAZUT

Riddle Me This

Match the questions (1 to 8) to the answers (A to H) to complete eight whimsical riddles.

Answers, page 167

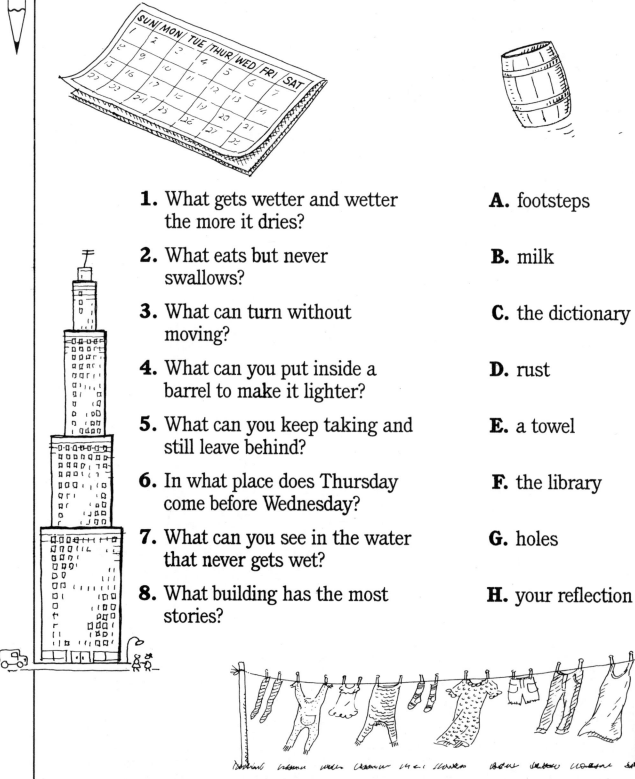

1. What gets wetter and wetter the more it dries?

2. What eats but never swallows?

3. What can turn without moving?

4. What can you put inside a barrel to make it lighter?

5. What can you keep taking and still leave behind?

6. In what place does Thursday come before Wednesday?

7. What can you see in the water that never gets wet?

8. What building has the most stories?

A. footsteps

B. milk

C. the dictionary

D. rust

E. a towel

F. the library

G. holes

H. your reflection

ILLUSTRATION BY PLATO TELEPOROS

Takeaway Games

The games on this page are for two players. In each game, players take turns coloring in one or more circles (no one may pass his or her turn). The winner of each game is the player who colors in the last circle in the game.

    Note: These games can also be played with coins (or other small objects). On a table, place coins in the same arrangements as the circles; then, instead of coloring in circles, players take turns removing coins. The player who removes the last coin is the winner.

NIM (invented by Charles Bouton in 1902)

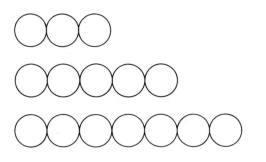

Rules: Players take turns coloring in any number of circles in any one row. The player to color in the last circle wins.

TRIANGULAR NIM

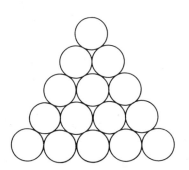

Rules: Players take turns coloring in any number of circles that lie in any straight line. The circles colored in a turn do not have to touch each other. The player to color in the last circle wins.

TSIANSHIDI (invented by W. A. Wythoff in 1907)

Rules: Players take turns coloring in either any number of circles in one row or an equal number of circles in both rows. The player to color in the last circle wins.

CROSSCRAM (invented by James Bynum in 1972)

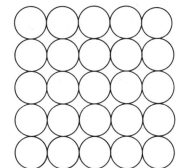

Rules: Players take turns coloring in any number of circles that lie next to each other in a straight line. One player may only color sets of circles lying in rows, while the other player may only color sets of circles lying in columns. Either player may use a turn to color a single circle (since a single circle is part of both a row and a column). The player to color in the last circle wins.

Variations

For additional challenges, try either or both of these rule changes:
1. Increase the number of circles in each game. In Nim, you can also try adding more rows.
2. Change the object of each game so that whoever colors in the last circle (or takes the last coin) *loses*.

The Olden Daze

"This antiques shop sure has interesting stuff in it," said Junior.

"Yeah," replied Jeannie, "but I wish things were labeled correctly. Each one has three descriptions on its tag."

"Oh, that's a little game I play," said a small voice from the corner. The kids hadn't even noticed the old woman sitting there. "I give my customers a 50% discount on the items they identify correctly."

Junior and Jeannie could have bought seven of the 12 items below at half-price. How many can you label correctly?

Answers, page 167

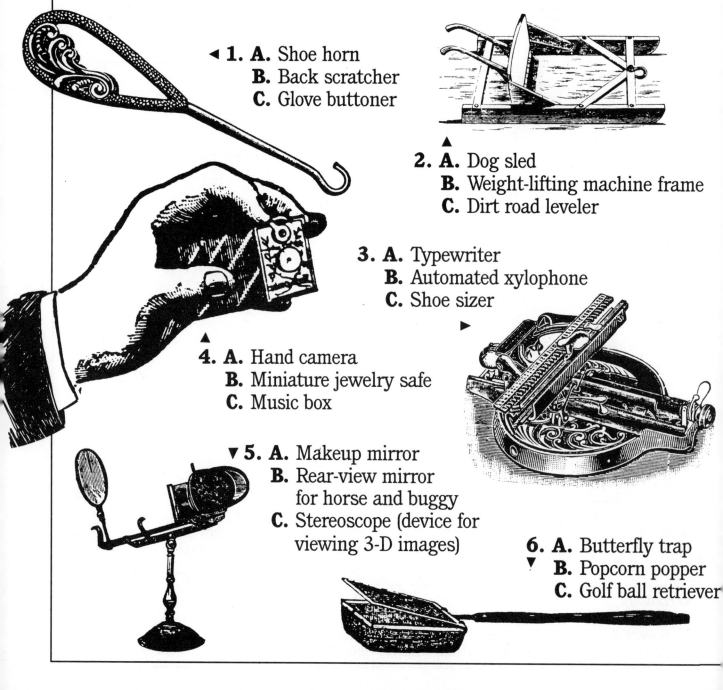

◄ **1. A.** Shoe horn
   B. Back scratcher
   C. Glove buttoner

▲
2. A. Dog sled
   B. Weight-lifting machine frame
   C. Dirt road leveler

3. A. Typewriter
   B. Automated xylophone
   C. Shoe sizer ►

▲
4. A. Hand camera
   B. Miniature jewelry safe
   C. Music box

▼ **5. A.** Makeup mirror
   B. Rear-view mirror
      for horse and buggy
   C. Stereoscope (device for
      viewing 3-D images)

6. A. Butterfly trap
▼ **B.** Popcorn popper
   C. Golf ball retriever

7. A. Ball for brewing tea leaves
   B. Locket for a necklace
   C. Perfume container
▼

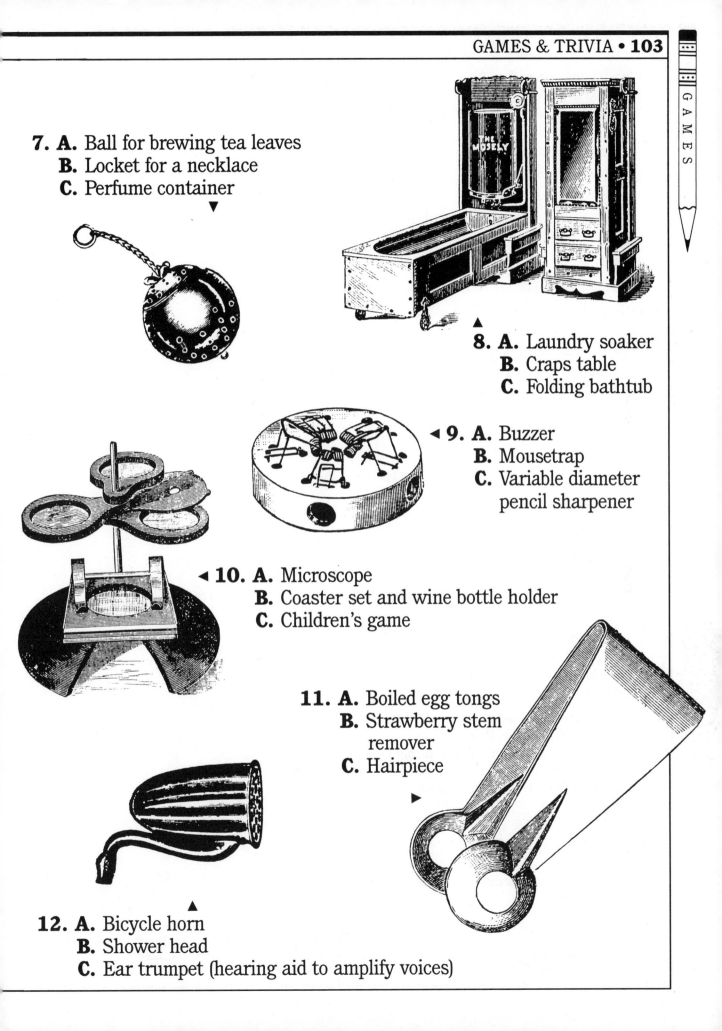

8. A. Laundry soaker
   B. Craps table
   C. Folding bathtub

◀ **9. A.** Buzzer
   B. Mousetrap
   C. Variable diameter
      pencil sharpener

◀ **10. A.** Microscope
     B. Coaster set and wine bottle holder
     C. Children's game

11. A. Boiled egg tongs
     B. Strawberry stem
       remover
     C. Hairpiece
▶

12. A. Bicycle horn
     B. Shower head
     C. Ear trumpet (hearing aid to amplify voices)

Can You Guess?

You're not expected to know the answers to these questions. Just give your best guess.

Answers, page 167

1. How many bones are there in the human body?
___ 50
___ 107
___ 206
___ more than 300

2. The stegosaur, a 30-foot dinosaur, weighed between four and six tons. Its brain, however, did not weigh quite that much. How much did the stegosaur's brain weigh?
___ 2½ ounces
___ 9 ounces
___ 1 pound
___ 5 pounds
___ 10 pounds

3. How far can a grasshopper travel in a single leap?
___ 2 feet
___ 5 feet
___ 10 feet
___ more than 15 feet

4. By the time the average American turns 70 years old, he or she will have eaten how many chickens?
___ 187
___ 1,050
___ 2,190
___ 4,090

5. Today the average baseball player's salary is over $370,000 per year. How much was baseball great Babe Ruth's salary during his starting year in 1914, when he played for the Baltimore Orioles of the International League?
___ $100
___ $600
___ $1,700
___ $5,890

6. How many distinct muscles are there in an elephant's trunk?
___ 25
___ 700
___ 18,900
___ more than 30,000

Play Ball!

First, write the answers to the baseball questions on the left in the circles that follow. Then, use a ruler to draw a straight line between the small dots on each pair of circles that contain matching numbers. We've done the first one as an example.

Each line will go through one of the letters in the middle of the page. Copy the letters that the lines cross onto the spaces at the bottom of the page, keeping them in the same order as the questions they go with. The result will be the answer to the baseball riddle below. *Answers, page 167*

What is the number of . . .

1. . . . strikes in an out?

2. . . . innings in a game?

3. . . . fingers on a fielder's mitt?

4. . . . bases on a field?

5. . . . games in a double-header?

6. . . . balls in play at once?

7. . . . the inning to stretch?

8. . . . men on base after a homer?

Letters: R, F, E, L, C, W, O, Z, B, J, N, D, A, L, L, G

Circle numbers: 3, 4, 3, 0, 5, 2, 9, 1, 7

Baseball Riddle
WHY DID DONALD DUCK AND DAISY DUCK WEAR THEIR DANCING SHOES TO THE BASEBALL GAME? BECAUSE THEY HEARD THERE WOULD BE A... _ _ _ _   _ _ _ _ !
1 2 3 4   5 6 7 8

Which Came First?

You've probably heard the question "Which came first, the chicken or the egg?" We don't know the answer to that question, but we do know, thanks to Joseph Kane's excellent book *Famous First Facts,* some other interesting firsts.

    Below, we have listed pairs of inventions, feats, facts, etc. In each case, can you correctly place a check mark by the one that came first?

Answers, page 167

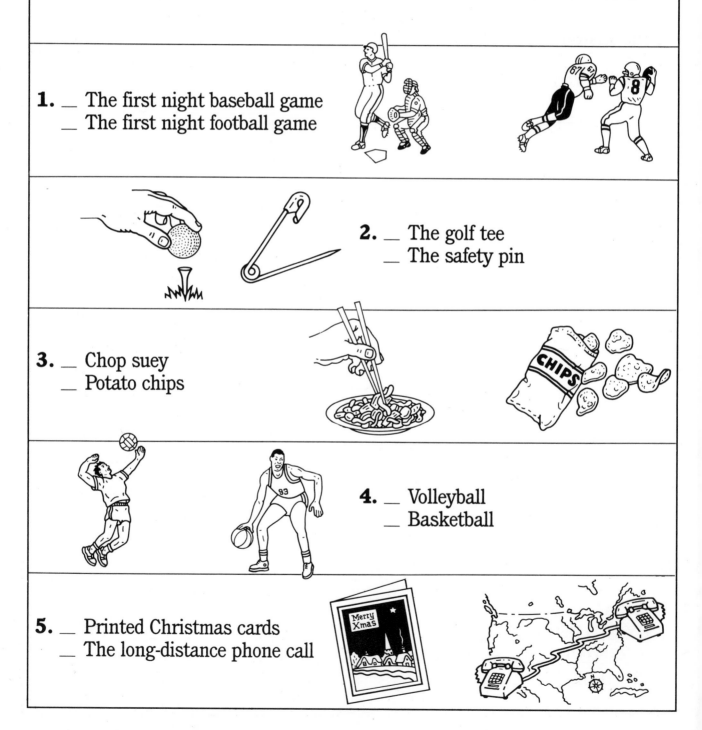

1. __ The first night baseball game
   __ The first night football game

2. __ The golf tee
   __ The safety pin

3. __ Chop suey
   __ Potato chips

4. __ Volleyball
   __ Basketball

5. __ Printed Christmas cards
   __ The long-distance phone call

GATE 10

6. __ The first cow to have flown and been milked in an airplane
__ The birth of the first reindeer in the United States

7. __ The automobile road map
__ The postage stamp catalog

8. __ The derby hat
__ Earmuffs

9. __ The ball-point pen
__ The pencil with attached eraser

10. __ Comic books
__ The bottle cap with cork liner

11. __ The first woman to swim the English Channel
__ The first airline stewardess

12. __ The 5¢ piece, or "nickel"
__ The parking meter

GAMES

Alaska? I'll Ask Ya!

Although the United States bought Alaska from Russia in 1867, Alaska didn't become a state until 1959.

Alaska is a land of many extremes: It is our largest state, boasts the highest peak on the continent (Mt. McKinley), contains vast oil fields, and is home to a great variety of wildlife not found elsewhere in the United States.

See how well you know the 49th state by answering the following questions.

Answers, page 168

1. Which one of the following facts about Alaska is false?
  a. Its 1985 population was approximately equal to the population of Cleveland, Ohio.
  b. California could fit inside it more than three and one-half times.
  c. Ice fields cover 49% of it.
  d. It contains both the easternmost and westernmost points in the United States.

2. What are Haida, Tlingit, and Tsimshian?
  a. Languages, other than English, that are spoken in Alaska.
  b. The three Alaskan sled dogs who have won the most races.
  c. The names of three Eskimo dances.
  d. The first great fishing boats to be used off the coast of Alaska.

3. The largest nugget found in the Alaskan gold rush weighed...
  a. 1.1 ounces
  b. 6.6 ounces
  c. 1.1 pounds
  d. 6.6 pounds

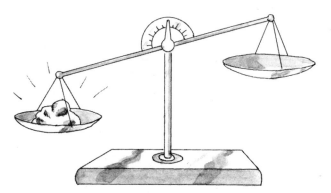

4. Alaska's flag was designed by 13-year-old Benny Benson in 1926, and was officially adopted when Alaska became a state. Which of these is Alaska's flag?

A   **B**   **C**   **D**

5. Except for a few (rarely sighted) garter snakes, no reptiles live in Alaska. True or False?

6. What is an Alaskan igloo made of?
   a. snow and ice
   b. snow, ice, and blubber
   c. snow, ice, blubber, and driftwood
   d. driftwood, whalebone, and sod

7. Which one of the following facts about polar bears is false?
   a. Their hair is actually transparent—refraction of light makes it appear whitish.
   b. They are so well insulated that infrared photography, which reveals heat, shows only their footprints.
   c. Although adult bears can weigh up to 2,000 pounds, babies weigh barely one pound at birth.
   d. They have been spotted as far south as Niagara Falls.

8. It costs about half as much to live in Alaska as it does to live in New York City. True or False?

9. The Arctic Circle, which cuts through approximately the top third of Alaska, is the line which marks . . .
   a. The southernmost point reached by glaciers in the last ice age.
   b. The areas of land habitable by arctic animals.
   c. The latitude at which the sun does not set at the summer solstice and does not rise at the winter solstice.
   d. The latitude at which the sun does not set at the winter solstice and does not rise at the summer solstice.

WRITTEN BY KAREN ANDERSON/ILLUSTRATIONS BY MIKE McCANN

What's in a Game?

How much do you know about games? If you think the answer is "not much," you may find some interesting surprises in the answers to this quiz. On each blank space, write the letter that matches the correct answer. Each choice (A, B, C, or D) will be used once in each question. *Answers, page 168*

1. Which spaces on a Monopoly board match these definitions?

___ According to computer-aided studies, this is the property that is landed on the most often.

___ This space is also the name of a game by Parker Brothers.

___ If you draw a certain Chance card, you may have to "take a walk" on this space.

___ If you land on this space on your first turn of the game, you have to pay $150.

A. Boardwalk   **B.** Free Parking   **C.** Illinois Avenue   **D.** Income Tax

2. What type of equipment is used to play each of these games?

___ Battleships
___ Fours
___ Giveaway
___ Klondike

A. cards   **B.** checker set   **C.** dominoes   **D.** paper and pencil

3. What numbers match these definitions?

___ a common winning total in a game of darts
___ the fastest anyone has thrown a Frisbee, in miles per hour
___ the highest number on any Bingo card
___ the most players ever in a Twister contest

A. 74   **B.** 75   **C.** 301   **D.** 4,034

4. Some games have different names in different countries. Names of other games sometimes change as time goes by. What is a more familiar name for each of these games?

___ draughts
___ noughts and crosses
___ pipopipette
___ reversi

A. dots-and-boxes   **B.** checkers   **C.** Othello   **D.** tic-tac-toe

WRITTEN BY WAYNE SCHMITTBERGER

States of Confusion

Each of the shapes below matches the shape of one of the states in the U.S.
To make them harder to recognize, we've turned some of them upside down
or sideways. We've also changed their sizes, so that some of the large states
appear to be small, and some of the small states appear large. How many of
the 16 different state shapes can you identify? *Answers, page 168*

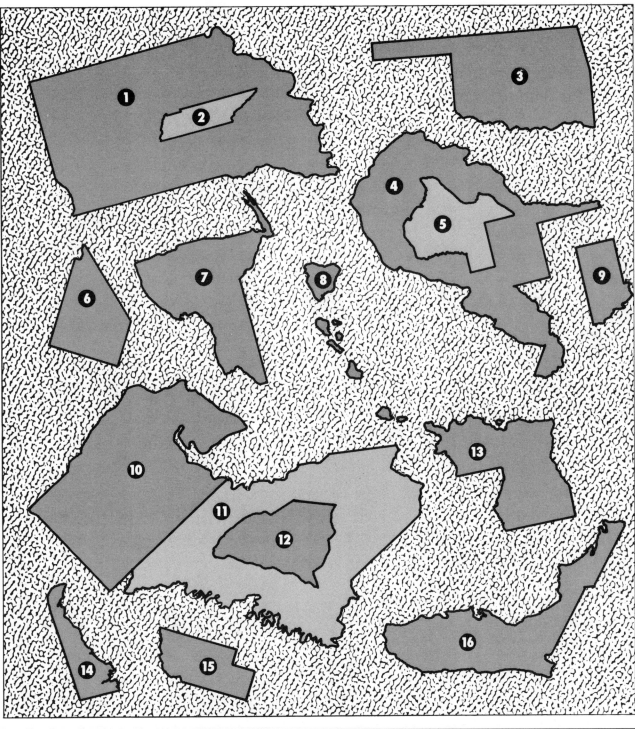

Who Was It?

Often, an inventor will give his name to his invention, or to companies that manufacture what he invented. Or, sometimes, an inventor can be forgotten, or remembered mainly for other accomplishments. Can you choose which person in each pair below invented the item or items named? If you're not sure, take your best guess. You're not expected to know all the names (especially since we made some of them up!).

Answers, page 169

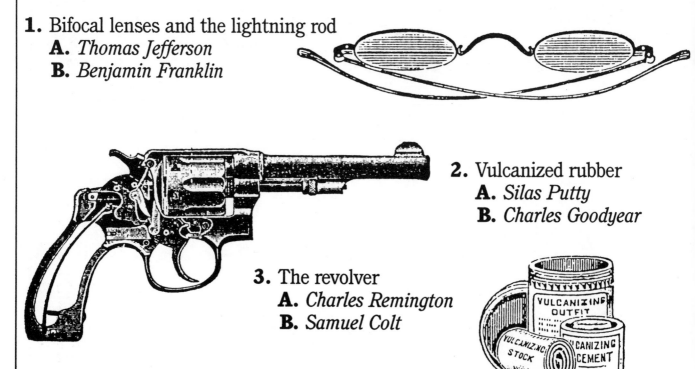

1. Bifocal lenses and the lightning rod
   A. *Thomas Jefferson*
   B. *Benjamin Franklin*

2. Vulcanized rubber
   A. *Silas Putty*
   B. *Charles Goodyear*

3. The revolver
   A. *Charles Remington*
   B. *Samuel Colt*

4. The metal detector
   A. *Eli Whitney*
   B. *Alexander Graham Bell*

5. Braille
   A. *Louis Braille*
   B. *Peter Reid*

6. Condensed milk
   A. *Gail Borden*
   B. *Louis Pasteur*

7. The electric razor
   A. *Jacob Schick*
   B. *King Camp Gillette*

8. The phonograph and
   the ticker-tape machine
   A. *Thomas Edison*
   B. *Victor Victrola*

9. The cylinder lock
   A. *Lloyd Master*
   B. *Linus Yale*

10. The fountain pen
   A. *Louis Waterman*
   B. *Robert Bic*

11. The mercury thermometer
   A. *Anders Celsius*
   B. *Gabriel Fahrenheit*

12. Dynamite
   A. *Giovanni Inferno*
   B. *Alfred Nobel*

13. The steel plow
   A. *John Deere*
   B. *Elias Howe*

14. The elevator
   A. *Otis Riser*
   B. *Elisha Otis*

WRITTEN BY KAREN ANDERSON

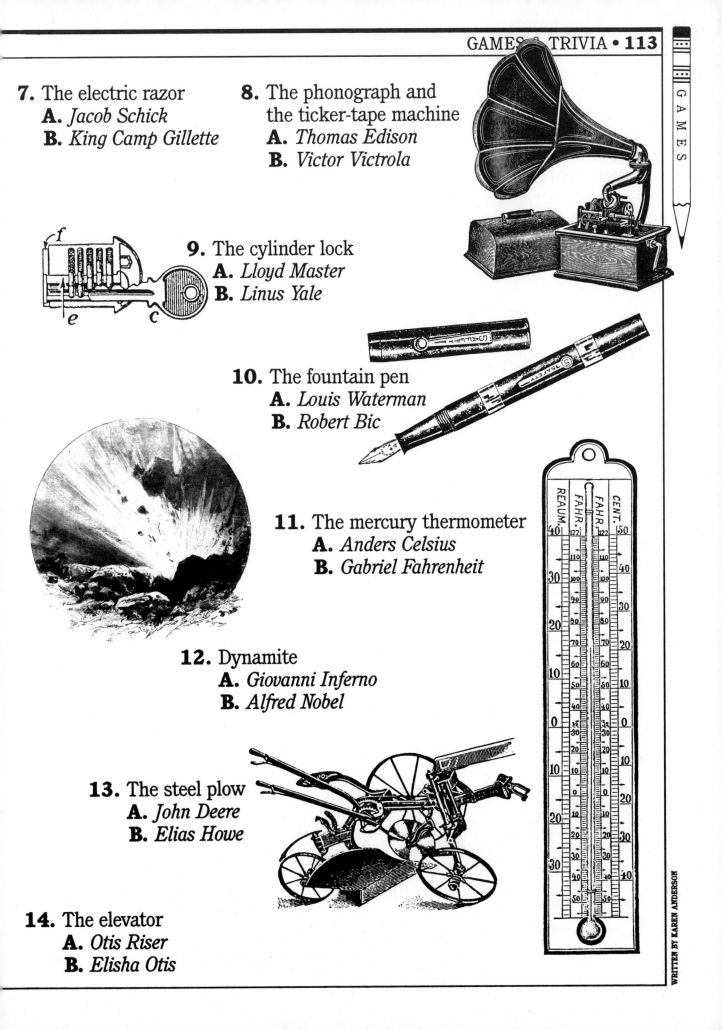

Twelve Tough Teasers

Some of these brainteasers have baffled the best puzzle solvers for years. Now it's your turn to get stumped.

Answers, page 169

1 Can you copy this figure on another piece of paper without retracing your path or lifting your pencil off the paper?

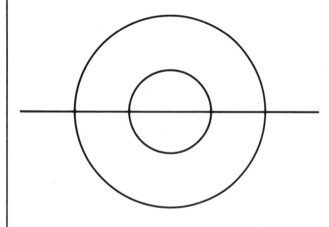

2 Jack tells Jill, "This isn't the $5 bill you left on the table. I found it between pages 15 and 16 of GAMES *Junior* magazine."

"You're lying," says Jill, "and I can prove it." How can Jill be sure?

3 If a train is one mile long, and is traveling at a speed of one mile per minute, how long will it take the train to go through a tunnel that is one mile long?

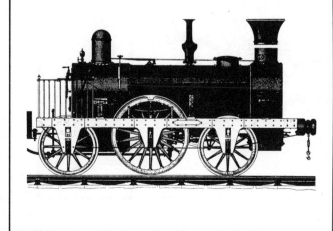

4 A certain day was "yesterday" when the day before yesterday was "yesterday." On that certain day, Kim's parents told her, "We'll go on a picnic the day after tomorrow if it doesn't rain tomorrow." It rained the day before yesterday, but not since. Did the family go on the picnic?

5 In a dish of red, yellow, and green M&M's candy, all but four are red, all but four are yellow, and all but four are green. How many M&M's are in the dish all together?

6 I have 10 U.S. coins worth a total of $1.19. But if you give me a dollar bill, it's impossible for me to give you exactly a dollar's worth of change in return. If one of my coins is a half-dollar, what are the other nine coins?

7 In Egypt, is a man allowed to marry his widow's sister?

8 Can you place an X in six different squares in this grid in such a way that no row, column, or diagonal has more than one X in it?

9 Here's the same grid, but with two if its corner squares removed. If you have 17 dominoes, each of which will cover exactly two squares in the grid, is it possible to place the dominoes on the grid in such a way that every square is completely covered?

10 Can you rearrange the letters in the word NOMINATES to make the name of one of the United States?

11 Using three toothpicks, it's easy to make an "equilateral" triangle, which is a triangle that has three equal sides. It's also possible—but not at all easy—to make *four* equilateral triangles by using only *six* toothpicks. Can you figure out how? Hint: You may need some glue.

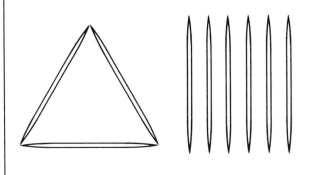

12 This classic brainteaser is very difficult. Three men registered at a hotel and paid 10 dollars each for one large room. After they had gone to their room, the hotel manager discovered that the men should have been charged only $25. The manager sent the bellboy to return $5 to the three men. But the bellboy, who was dishonest, returned only $3 to the men, and kept the other $2 himself.

   The men originally spent $30, but they got back $3, so in all they spent $27. The bellboy kept $2. This makes a total of $29. But the three men had originally paid out $30.Where was the missing dollar?

Cats Incredible!

A recent survey found that cats are now more popular than dogs as pets. If you're a cat lover, or if you're just curious about why cats are so well-liked, we think you will enjoy this quiz.

Answers, page 170

1. Cats are known by similar names in different languages. Match the language (a–h) to its word for "cat" (1–8).

a. Greek	**1.** *mao*
b. Spanish	**2.** *qittah*
c. German	**3.** *chat*
d. Ancient Egyptian	**4.** *kata*
e. Arabic	**5.** *katze*
f. Russian	**6.** *miu*
g. French	**7.** *gato*
h. Chinese	**8.** *koshka*

2. Because of genetic mutations, certain cats often inherit odd traits. Which one of the following statements is false?
  a. Most calico cats are female.
  b. White cats, especially those with blue eyes, are often deaf.
  c. Burmese cats often have six or more toes.
  d. Siamese cats are frequently cross-eyed.

3. It only takes one-eighth of a second for a cat to right itself when it is falling upside down. True or False?

4. Which one of the following names is *not* a breed of cat?
  a. Ragdoll
  b. Lavender
  c. Chartreux
  d. Maine Coon
  e. Jasper
  f. Havana Brown
  g. Korat

5. Cats were first kept as pets about 2,000 years ago (around the year 0). True or False?

6. Cats are color blind. True or False?

7. Whiskers help a cat to:
   a. judge if it can fit through an opening
   b. locate scraps of food on the ground
   c. sense objects in the dark by feeling air currents
   d. all of the above

8. Most cats are left-handed (left-pawed). True or False?

9. One of the following statements about cats is false. Which one?
   a. Cats get stuck up trees because, although they are well adapted for climbing, if they were to come down head first, like squirrels, they would be unbalanced and fall.
   b. Cats seem more independent and antisocial than dogs because their relatives are loners, whereas dogs and their ancestors hunt in packs.
   c. Cats sometimes tear around the house to express their instinctive need to chase and hunt prey.
   d. Cats can see in total darkness by using infrared vision to sense warm objects, as some reptiles do.
   e. Cats often don't feel pain from heat until their hair is singed.

10. Match the breed of cat (a–e) to its picture (1–5).
   a. Siamese
   b. Rex
   c. Manx
   d. Persian
   e. Russian Blue

WRITTEN BY KAREN ANDERSON/ILLUSTRATIONS BY JUAN BARBERIS

What's the Difference?

For each set of items below, we *were* going to ask you to tell us which one doesn't belong with the other two. But then we realized that no matter what answer you gave, you would be right! That's because there's something about each item that makes it different from the other two things in the same group. In the first group, for example, you could say that the penny is different because of its color—but you could also say that the nickel is different because it's tail-side up, or that the dime is different (how?). Can you figure out what's different about each object in the four other groups?

Answers, page 170

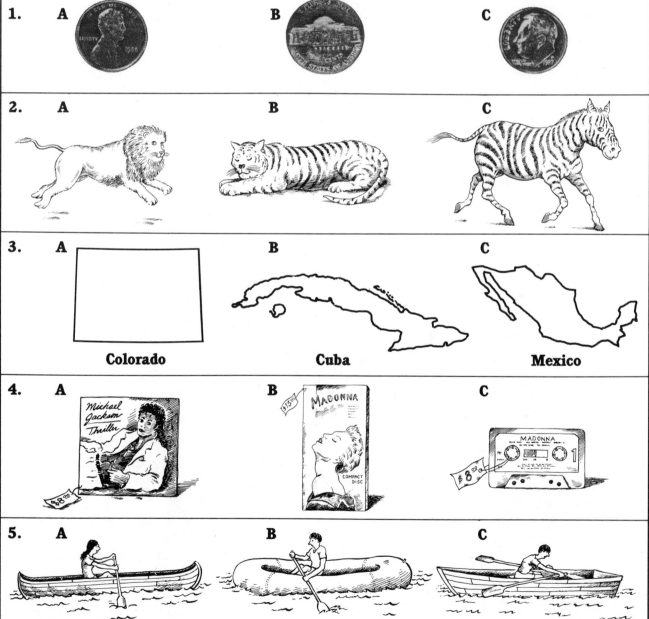

High-Low Quiz

A time machine magically carries you back to any year you choose. Each time you stop, you are offered something for sale at a certain price. It is up to you to guess whether the price is too high or too low, compared to the usual price at that time. What do you think?

Answers, page 170

1 It is 1987. (Your time machine is still warming up.) You can buy a compact disc of Madonna's *True Blue*. The price is $2.75.

High __ Low __

2 It is 1952. You are offered a Baby Ruth candy bar for 25¢.

High __ Low __

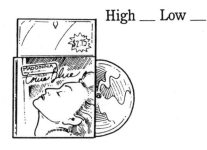

3 It is 1982. A sports fan offers to sell you a complete set of the year's Topps baseball cards. All 792 cards can be had for $13.65.

High __ Low __

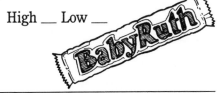

4 It is 1959. You can purchase a copy of *MAD* magazine for 75¢.

High __ Low __

5 It is 1961. You can purchase a genuine wallet-size color photo of rock and TV star Ricky Nelson for 25¢.

High __ Low __

6 It is 1976. Someone offers to take you on an around-the-world cruise aboard the Queen Elizabeth II. You are going to travel in the most luxurious manner possible, and you are going to be roomed in absolutely the best suite available. The cost for such a cruise in the grandest style will be $52,000.

High __ Low __

7 It is 1959 again. You can buy a famous four-blade Scout pocket knife. It features steel blades to open cans and bottles, to punch holes, and to drive screws. The price for this fabulous knife is 75¢.

High __ Low __

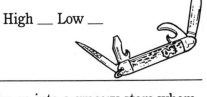

8 It is 1948. You go into a grocery store where you see a six-bottle carton of Coca-Cola selling for 50¢ plus deposit.

High __ Low __

GAMES

Travel Bingo

Game Card #1

This game is for two players (or two teams of players) who are riding in a car. The only equipment needed is two pencils or pens, and the two "game cards" on this page.

One player uses the top game card, and the other uses the bottom game card. When a player sees something out the car window that matches one of the squares on his or her card, the player calls its

name out loud, then marks off the matching square on the game card.

The object is to be the first player to mark off four squares in any straight line—that is, all the squares in any row, column, or long diagonal. Or, for a long trip, players may try to be first to mark off all 16 spaces. If neither player is able to do this, the player who marks off the most squares wins.

Game Card #2

WRITTEN BY WAYNE SCHMITTBERGER/ILLUSTRATIONS BY TED ENIK

4

Mystery, Logic & Numbers

Out of Order 1

The panels of this comic strip are all mixed up. Can you unscramble the pictures so that they tell a story?

Answer, page 170

A

B

C

D

E

F

PUZZLE AND ILLUSTRATIONS BY ROBERT LEIGHTON

The Perfect Match

This trick uses only 10 cards from a standard deck: the 4, 5, 6, 7, and 8 of spades, and the 4, 5, 6, 7, and 8 of hearts. But even after you learn how to do it, you'll probably still be amazed that it works.

Stack the 10 cards in the order shown at the bottom of the page.

Now, turn the stack of cards face down, and cut them wherever you like. Then, remove the top five cards and place them in a separate stack on the table. Turn the other five cards face up and place them to the left of the first stack. You now have two stacks of five cards each, one face up and one face down, as the picture shows.

Next, you will spell "WILL THE CARDS MATCH?" using the following directions to reorder the cards as you wish.

To spell WILL, choose either pile and put one card from the top to the bottom of the pile for W. For I, again pick either stack and transfer one card from top to bottom. Similarly, use either pile to transfer cards for each L.

Now remove the top card from each pile and place this pair out of the way. (Keep one card in this pair face down, and the other face up.)

Next, spell THE using the two piles (which now have four cards each), again choosing either pile for each letter, and transferring one card from front to back for each of the letters T, H, and E.

Again remove the top card from each pile and put this pair beside the first pair you removed.

Spell the word CARDS using the same method. Then place the top two cards beside the other two pairs.

For the last word, you have two cards left in two piles. Spell MATCH, again switching a card in either pile from top to bottom for each letter. Pick the top two cards off, keeping them together, and put the last two cards together.

You now have five pairs of randomly chosen cards, with one card in each pair face down. For the grand finale, turn over the face-down card in each pair. You will have five pairs of matching cards!

Detective's Notebook

File: Crime Solving
Case: 1

"I came as fast as I could, sergeant," Officer Fred Dumpty stood panting in the doorway to Sergeant Rider's office.

Dumpty had been called to the office in the middle of a quick bite, and sugar powder from a doughnut coated the front of his uniform.

"Close the door, Dumpty, and clean off your uniform," said Rider gruffly, from behind his desk. "I've told you to pay more attention to your appearance."

Rider was furious; but Dumpty soon found out that it wasn't only because of Dumpty's uniform. In a low voice seething with anger, Rider said, "We managed to capture Bart Hargrove and brought him here until federal officers arrive."

"That's great!" cried Dumpty. "He's wanted in four states. The mayor will give you a commendation."

"No, you idiot, he'll probably fire me: Hargrove has just escaped. It'll cost me my badge."

Though the sergeant often criticized Dumpty, he wasn't a bad guy and needed Dumpty's help. "Do we have any clues?" asked Dumpty.

"We have a report that a man fitting Hargrove's description stole a motorscooter and headed east not more than 20 minutes ago."

"He can't get very far," said Dumpty. "If he's headed east, I can overtake him. But what does he look like?"

Sergeant Rider handed him a wanted poster. "Too bad this isn't a clear picture. But since Hargrove is as bald as a honeydew melon and is wearing prison clothes, he should be easy to recognize."

Rider groaned. "Not any more. He stole an officer's street clothes from his locker, then shoplifted another outfit from a

WRITTEN BY MARVIN MILLER/ILLUSTRATION BY PHIL SCHEUER

clothing store. We don't know what he's wearing now."

"Sounds bad, but I'm glad you have confidence in me to find him, Sarge."

"Don't call me Sarge," barked Rider, who did everything by the book. "And by the way, you're not finding anybody, I am—you're driving me."

In the police car, Dumpty told Rider that the motorscooter couldn't have traveled more than 10 miles. "The farthest he could have got is Dover City." Minutes later, they arrived at the outskirts of town. As he passed Walden's General Store, Dumpty put on the brakes. There was a motorscooter in the parking lot.

"Wait in the car while I check out the store," said Rider. "Maybe Hargrove stopped to buy food."

"Say, Sergeant, could you buy me a bag of potato chips while you're in there? I haven't eaten lunch yet."

"Do you ever stop thinking about food, Dumpty? Buy it yourself."

Dumpty happily followed Rider into the store. Inside, Rider spotted a suspicious-looking man at the checkout counter. He was wearing a big hat pulled down tight over his head. He seemed to fit the description of Hargrove. "Dumpty," whispered Rider triumphantly from behind a display rack, "he must be Hargrove. He put on a hat to cover his bald head—why else would he be wearing a hat inside the store? I'm going to arrest him." He started to pull out his revolver.

"Buutseerg . . ."

"What did you say, Dumpty?"

Behind him, Dumpty swallowed the potato chips he had been eating (he was going to

pay for them at the counter). "But Sarge, I think you're making a big mistake."

Rider's face turned red. "Who cares what you think? Look at you, potato chips all over your uniform. A cop who doesn't pay attention to appearances isn't much of a cop."

Dumpty simply smiled and whispered something into

Rider's ear. "As much as I hate to admit it, I guess you're right, Dumpty. He's not our man. Let's continue into town before Bart Hargrove gets much farther."

ON THE FACING PAGE IS A PICTURE OF OFFICER DUMPTY AND SERGEANT RIDER INSIDE THE GENERAL STORE. HOW DID DUMPTY KNOW THE MAN WASN'T BART HARGROVE?

Answer, page 170

File: Stakeout
Category: Lip Reading

Some detectives read lips to learn valuable information. While on a stakeout, a detective saw several suspicious persons enter a guarded door. Each was allowed inside by using a secret password that changed daily.

Below is what the detective saw through her telescope dur-

ing the six days of her stakeout. She took a picture of the person's lips just as the person was starting to pronounce the secret password.

Can you match the pictures (1–6) with the following passwords (A–F)?

Answers, page 170

A–EAGLE   C–OOZE   E—APPLE
B–MICROFILM   D–THREAD   F–SHADOW

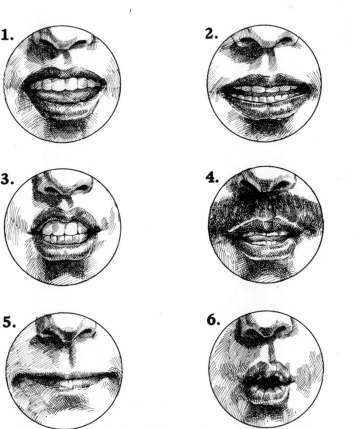

The Dating Game

While he was snooping in his sister's room, Junior found these six pages from a date book on her desk. He was disappointed that he didn't find anything he could threaten to tell Mom and Dad about, but he did have fun putting the pages back into their correct order. Can you rearrange the six pages so that they are in chronological order?

Answers, page 170

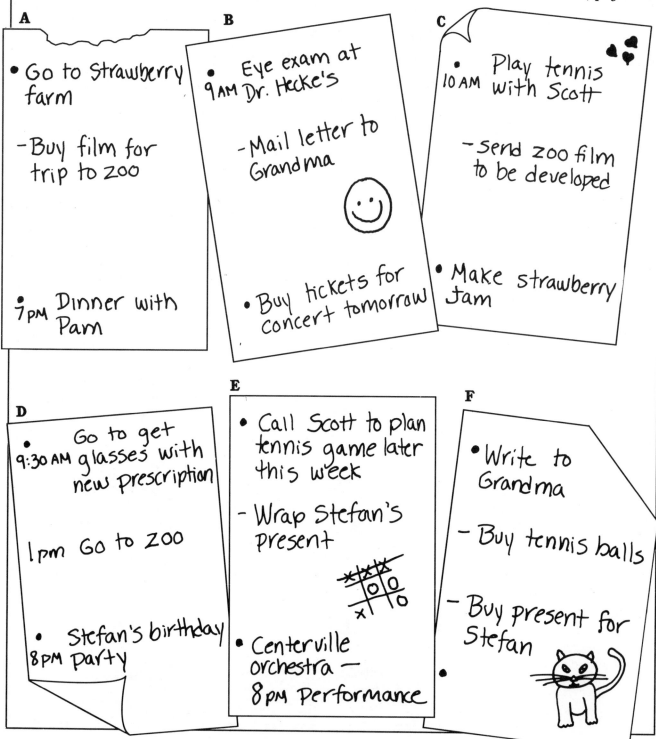

A
- Go to Strawberry farm
- Buy film for trip to zoo
- 7 PM Dinner with Pam

B
- Eye exam at 9 AM Dr. Hecke's
- Mail letter to Grandma
- Buy tickets for concert tomorrow

C
- 10 AM Play tennis with Scott
- Send zoo film to be developed
- Make strawberry jam

D
- 9:30 AM Go to get glasses with new prescription
- 1 pm Go to zoo
- 8 PM Stefan's birthday party

E
- Call Scott to plan tennis game later this week
- Wrap Stefan's present
- Centerville orchestra — 8 PM Performance

F
- Write to Grandma
- Buy tennis balls
- Buy present for Stefan

PUZZLE BY KAREN ANDERSON

Work Boxes

Fill in the Work Boxes at the bottom of the page by following the instructions below and using the boxes given. Take your time to think about each step.

Answers, page 170

Boxes

a	b	c	d	e	f	g	h	i	j
8	5	10	3	6	4	2	9	7	1

(H) (E) (R) (N) (A) (L) (T) (W) (I) (D)

1 Add the number in box i to the number in box g. Place the result in Work Box e.

2 Subtract the number in box i from the number in box c. Place the result in Work Box g.

3 If the number in box b is odd, go to step 5.

4 Add the number in box i to the number in box b. Place the result in Work Box d.

5 Subtract the number in box j from the number in box a. Place the result in Work Box f.

6 Repeat the instructions for #2, but place the result in Work Box h.

7 Subtract the number in box d from the number in box b. Place the result in Work Box a.

8 Divide the number in box c by the number in box g. Place the result in Work Box i.

9 Multiply the number in box f by the number in box g. Place the result in Work Box b.

10 Repeat the instructions in #8, but place the result in Work Box c.

11 Add the number in box g to the number in box a. Place the result in Work Box j.

Now, in the circle below each Work Box, write the letter that appears below the *same* number at the top of the page. If a Work Box is empty, do not write a letter below it.

If you have followed all the directions correctly, you will find a phrase that describes you!

Work Boxes

a	b	c	d	e	f	g	h	i	j

PUZZLE BY JEANNE KOLLAR

Out of Order 2

The panels of this comic strip are all mixed up. Can you unscramble the pictures so that they tell a story?

Answer, page 170

A   **B**   **C**

D   **E**   **F**

PUZZLE AND ILLUSTRATIONS BY ROBERT LEIGHTON

A Logical Treasure Hunt

The treasure map below was drawn by Captain Hood Winker, a pirate who loved puzzles as much as plunder. He buried a fortune in gold doubloons within one of the square areas (A through J) marked with an X.

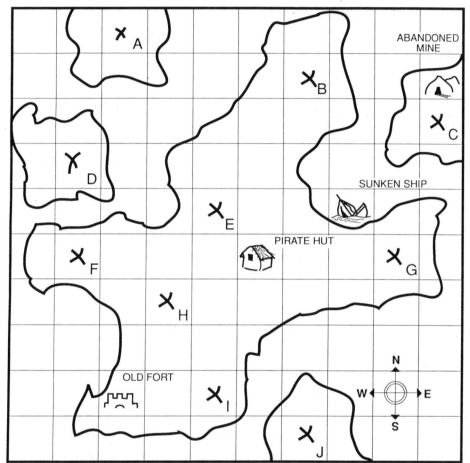

He also wrote these clues on the back of the map:

1. An even number of squares marked X are farther east than the treasure.

2. The treasure is not located at the X that is closest to the abandoned mine.

3. If there are an even number of Xs farther north than the treasure, the treasure is located on one of the four small islands.

4. If the treasure is on one of the four small islands, then the distance from the treasure to the nearest other X is greater than the distance from the pirate hut to the sunken ship.

5. If the treasure is on the big island, then one of the buildings is farther west than the treasure and the other building is farther north than the treasure.

Can you save a lot of digging by figuring out which X marks the treasure's location?

Answer, page 170

Coin Return

With this trick, you will be able to tell whether a coin hidden under a friend's hand has its "heads" or "tails" side up, even though your friend may have turned it over any number of times while you were not looking.

First, have your friend put a handful of coins on a table in such a way that all of them are visible. It doesn't matter how many coins are used, or how many have their heads or tails sides up.

Now turn your back, and tell your friend to turn over as many coins as he or she wishes, one coin at a time. Each time your friend turns a coin over, he or she is to call out "TURN." Your friend may even turn over the same coin more than once.

While you're still facing the other way, have your friend cover any one coin with his or her hand. Now turn around and look at the coins on the table. Almost immediately, you announce whether the coin hidden under your friend's hand is heads or tails.

Example
In the picture, if your secret number is even, the covered coin must be tails.

How the Trick Is Done
When the coins are first placed on the table, secretly count the number of heads-up coins. Then, each time your friend says "TURN," add one to this number, counting silently in your head until your friend is done. The number you end up with is your secret total.

If your secret total is an even number, there will be an even number of heads-up coins on the table. When you turn around, count the heads-up coins you see. If you see an odd number of heads, the coin covered by your friend's hand must be heads (to make the total even). If you see an even number of heads, the covered coin must be tails.

If your secret total is odd, there will be an odd number of heads-up coins on the table. So, in this case, if you see an even number of heads when you turn around, you know the hidden coin must be heads; while if you count an odd number of heads, the hidden coin must be tails.

WRITTEN BY MARVIN MILLER

What Comes Next?

Answer, page 171

G
A
M
E
S

Detective's Notebook

File: Crime Solving
Case: 2

Cruising through town early one morning, Officer Fred Dumpty felt grumpy. He was on a diet. For breakfast, Dumpty usually ate bacon and pancakes with plenty of syrup, a glass of milk, sausages, buttered toast, some orange juice, and a corn muffin. All he had had today was cereal with skim milk. "I ate 15 minutes ago and I'm hungry already. I'm never going to make it to lunch." Though he didn't do it on purpose, Dumpty soon found himself driving down Maple Street, toward an area of town that had a lot of restaurants. None of the restaurants were open yet and the sidewalks were empty.

As he passed Pulski's Restaurant, Dumpty noticed something strange and stopped the car. Outside the locked front door of Pulski's was stacked the morning's bakery delivery. Dumpty observed that several pies and cakes had been removed from their boxes, and that someone had taken big bites out of them. A large brown paper bag full of dinner rolls had been ripped apart and scattered across the pavement. On the sidewalk was a squashed lemon meringue pie. "Imagine ruining all this good food," Dumpty thought sadly. He grabbed his radio mike. "There's been some vandalism and theft at Pulski's. Better tell Mr. Pulski to come over quickly."

About 10 minutes later, the store owner arrived. "What a catastrophe!" he shouted. "Whoever did this should go to jail."

"Calm down, Mr. Pulski," said Dumpty. "I'm on the job, so you can be confident the case will be solved."

That statement did not seem to put Mr. Pulski's mind at ease. "This is the third incident this week," said the unhappy owner. "Monday someone squirted

ketchup across the front window. Tuesday we kept getting take-out orders over the phone for addresses that didn't exist. And now today, this."

Dumpty bent down and examined the squashed lemon meringue pie. A bicycle had ridden over it. One of its tires had left a short trail.

"I'll bet it's those Thomas kids," muttered Mr. Pulski. "I chased them away from the front of my restaurant a few days ago, but they kept riding by with their bikes and making noise, and they almost knocked down one of my customers." Mr. Pulski pointed in the direction of the tire track: "See. They live in that direction, a few miles down. Hey, Dumpty, you can get your nose out of the pie now and check on the kids . . . C'mon Dumpty, I'll give you a piece of cake if you're that hungry."

"No thanks," sighed the policeman, getting up, "I'm on a diet."

It wasn't long before Dumpty pulled up to the Thomas house. As he got out of the car, he heard noises coming from the open garage. There were Tim and Kim huddled over a bicycle.

"Where have you kids been for the last hour?" asked Dumpty. Tim nudged his sister with his elbow. Kim straightened up. "We've been cleaning my bike."

"Yeah," said Tim, "we've been cleaning her bike. Is that against the law?"

"Someone broke into bags of food in front of a restaurant on Maple Street," said Dumpty sternly. "Let me have a look at those tires."

"It wasn't us," said Tim. "We haven't been near Pulski's since Monday."

Dumpty examined the front

and back whitewall tires. The rear tire looked as if it had just been washed. It was still wet.

"How come you kids cleaned off just one of the tires?"

"Uhh, we were just about to do the front," said Tim.

"Uhh, we ran out of soap," said Kim at the same instant.

"Well, I think both of you are lying," said Dumpty. You were

the ones who vandalized Pulski's restaurant. And you cleaned the rear tire because it was covered with lemon meringue."

ON THE FACING PAGE IS A PICTURE OF OFFICER DUMPTY IN FRONT OF PULSKI'S RESTAURANT. HOW DID HE KNOW THE THOMAS KIDS WERE LYING?

Answers, page 171

File: Secret Messages 1
Category: Pigpen Code

The diagrams below are the key to a secret alphabet code you can use to send a hidden message. It's called a "pigpen code" because each letter is in a compartment, or pen, that has a unique shape.

To send your message, draw the outline of the compartment each letter is in, including a dot if there is one. For example, here is how to send the message "WATCH OUT":

Can you decipher this secret message?

Answers, page 171

File: Miscellaneous 1
Category: Top Secret

A small map (or a secret message) can be hidden inside a ballpoint pen. Roll the map tightly around the ink tube and slip it back inside the outer shell.

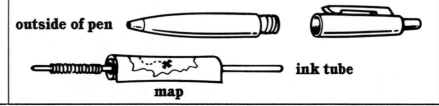

outside of pen

map   **ink tube**

Pack Magic

The Trick

Have each of four friends take a card, without seeing it, from different parts of a deck. When the four cards are turned over, they will all be aces!

How to Do It

Cut out or copy the four number cards shown below. Give a number card to each of four friends. (You can also do the trick with one friend, giving him or her all the cards, or give two cards each to two friends.)

Tell each person to secretly think of any one of the numbers on his or her card. Now, ask them to spell their numbers with a deck of cards, removing one card for each letter. Show them what you mean by spelling 20. Take one card off the top of the deck as you name each letter: T-W-E-N-T-Y, and hold onto the last card (the "Y" card). After this demonstration, return all six cards to the top of the deck. Have your friends count off their numbers in the order of their lettered cards: first the person with card A, then cards B, C, and D.

After person A spells his or her number and holds onto the last card, have him or her pass the remainder of the deck to person B. When B is done, pass it to C, and then to D.

Now have your friends look at their cards—they are all aces!

The Secret

Before you start, secretly arrange the deck so that the four aces are in positions 10, 21, 30, and 38, counting from the top of the deck. The trick will always work if you have each friend take his turn in the order of the letters written on the number cards. (A, B, C, and D)

NUMBER CARDS

A			B			C			D		
43	24	39	28	74	87	69	32	17	52	41	13
57	71	35	88	37	23	21	49	36	46	19	61
29	48	72	33	79	97	86	91	55	18	51	66
84	85	67	75	38	83	54	45	82	56	62	42

WRITTEN BY MARVIN MILLER

GAMES

Out of Order 3

The panels of this comic strip are all mixed up. Can you unscramble the pictures so that they tell a story?

Answer, page 171

A

B

C

D

E

F

PUZZLE AND ILLUSTRATIONS BY ROBERT LEIGHTON

Color Schemes

To make maps easy to read, they are often colored according to a rule that touching regions must always be colored differently. To color a large, complicated map this way, you might think you would need to use a lot of different colors. But in fact, you never need more than four colors, no matter what the map looks like.

The drawings below aren't maps, but the same principle applies to them. Can you find a way to color all the regions in each drawing, using no more than four different colors, so that regions of the same color never touch? Suggestion: Before coloring a pattern, plan how you will do it by penciling in the names of your chosen colors in each region. *Answers, page 171*

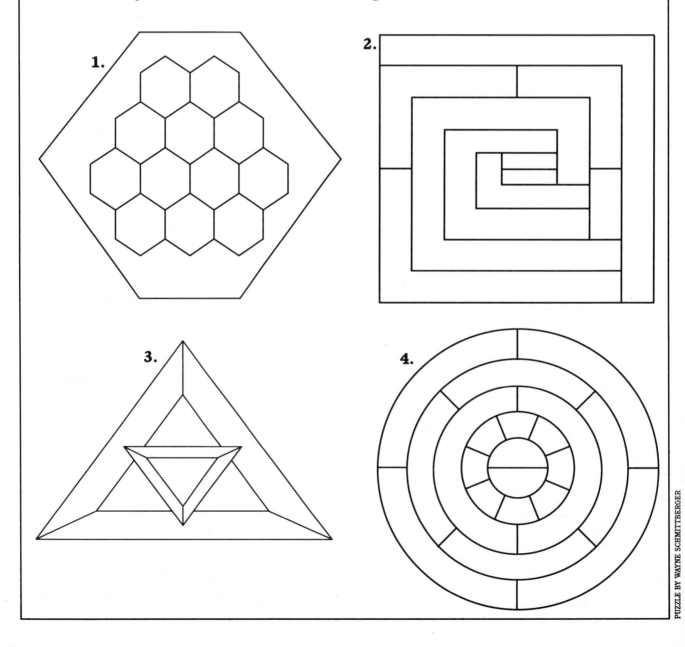

PUZZLE BY WAYNE SCHMITTBERGER

Lights Out!

The eight cave explorers in the top scene were having a good time until a gust of wind blew out their torches. When the light suddenly disappeared, people panicked and groped around in the dark to orient themselves.

    The bottom scene shows the dark cave, with balloons indicating what each person is saying. Can you deduce, by looking at the clues in the first scene, which person is saying each bit of dialogue in the second?

Answers, page 171

1 What...achoo! What happened?

2 I'm over here, Bill, follow the sound of my keys jingling.

3 Hey, my glasses fell off!

4 Don't worry, I have a flashlight in my backpack.

5 Oh, no, my torch went out!

6 Sandy, where are you?

7 Hold my hand tighter, I don't want to lose you.

8 Ow! I stubbed my toe.

PUZZLE BY MARVIN MILLER/ILLUSTRATION BY TED ENIK

Out of Order 4

The panels of this comic strip are all mixed up. Can you unscramble the pictures so that they tell a story?

Answer, page 171

A

B

C

D

E

F

PUZZLE AND ILLUSTRATION BY ROBERT LEIGHTON

Triviarithmetic

Fill in the blanks for clues A through O at the bottom. Transfer these numbers to the squares with the same letters in the grid. When you are done, each row and column will form a correct mathematical equation that should be solved from left to right or from top to bottom. Work backward from the grid to answer any clues you don't know.

Answers, page 171

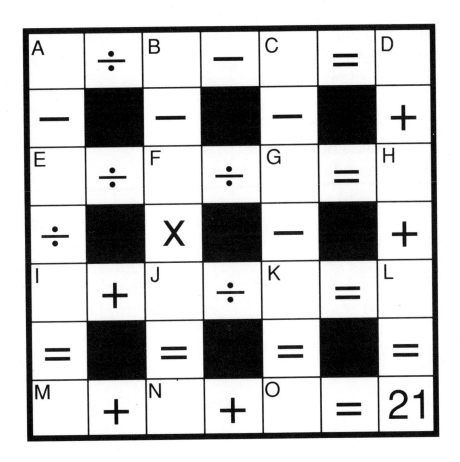

A Book: *The ___ Hats of Bartholomew Cubbins*

B Song: "___ Little Indians"

C Movie: *Miracle on ___th Street*

D Movie: *___ Candles*

E Book: *Around the World in ___ Days*

F TV show: *___ Is Enough*

G TV show: *Hawaii ___-O*

H Song: "A Bicycle Built for ___"

I TV show: *___ Minutes*

J Song: "___ Blind Mice"

K TV show: *___ Jump Street*

L Movie: *___ Men and a Baby*

M Movie: *Snow White and the ___ Dwarfs*

N TV show: *The ___ Million Dollar Man*

O Drink: V-___

The Magic Die

With this trick, you can prove to a friend that you have a magic die.

Deal out six blank cards (made from pieces of cardboard), and have your friend roll the die as many times as he or she likes. After the final roll, you will count out the number on the top face of the die, moving from card to card as you count. You will then place the die on the card where the counting stops.

When you turn over the other five cards, they will be blank. But when you turn over the card under the die, it will say, "You will pick this card."

How the Trick Is Done

Before starting the trick, take six blank pieces of cardboard and write "You will pick this card" on one of them. Arrange the cards so that the one marked with the message is the third from the top.

Deal out the cards in a line, from left to right. Remember that the card with the writing on it is now the third from your left.

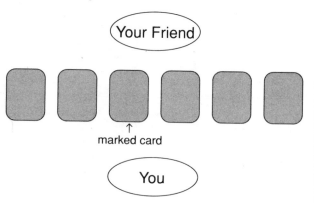

Your Friend

↑
marked card

You

After your friend has stopped rolling, and chosen a number, you will count out that number by using whatever method of counting will get you to the third card. The chart below will show you how.

If the number on the die is	Here's how you reach the card
1, 2, or 6	Spell O-N-E, T-W-O, or S-I-X, starting from your left.
3	Count 1, 2, 3, starting from your left.
4	Count 1, 2, 3, 4, starting from your right.
5	Spell F-I-V-E, starting from your right.

WRITTEN BY MARVIN MILLER

Square Deal

The line drawn through the square below passes through boxes totaling 19 (4 + 9 + 5 + 1). What is the *highest* total that you can make with one straight line?

Answer, page 171

The Magic Touch

With this trick, you can show a friend that you can feel whether the cards in a pack are face up or down.

Your friend shuffles a deck of 20 cards as much as he or she likes. Half of these cards should be face up, and half face down.

Then, your friend hands you the deck. You hold the cards behind your back and sort the deck into two piles, "feeling" the faces of the cards. You then produce two piles of 10 cards each. When your friend counts, each pile will have exactly the same number of upside-down cards!

How the Trick Is Done

Your friend can shuffle the 20 cards in any way, as long as none of the cards are turned over. (At all times, 10 should face up and 10 should face down.) When you take the cards behind your back, count off the top 10 cards and hold each pile of 10 in one hand. Before you bring the piles in front of you, turn one of the piles over. When you spread out the two stacks and count how many face-down cards are in each stack, the totals will always be the same.

WRITTEN BY MARVIN MILLER/ILLUSTRATION BY R. J. KAUFMAN

Out of Order 5

The panels of this comic strip are all mixed up. Can you unscramble the pictures so that they tell a story?

Answer, page 171

Lizard Logic

A secret admirer dropped a Valentine and a pet salamander into Amy's mailbox and she wants to know who he is. Three neighbors saw the boy, and each one told Amy two things about his appearance. But Amy's neighbors weren't sure if they approved of her admirer, so they each told her one fact and one lie about him. Keeping this in mind, can you deduce which of the eight possible admirers below gave Amy the amphibious Valentine?

Answer, page 171

1st Neighbor: "He had on a funny hat and wore strange glasses."
2nd Neighbor: "He had huge ears and did not wear glasses."
3rd Neighbor: "He had dark hair and no hat."

Abner   Boris   Calvin

Dennis   Elmer

Felix   Gomer   Horace

ILLUSTRATIONS BY STEVE MELLOR

5
Big Bad Toughies

Cross Numbers

This puzzle is like a crossword, except that it uses numbers instead of words. One digit must be placed in each box, forming a three-digit number in each column (reading down) and each row (reading left to right). Clues to these three-digit numbers are given below.

Here's one additional clue: Every digit from 1 through 9 will be used exactly once in the grid.

Answers, page 172

A has a first digit that is one less than its second digit, and a second digit that is one less than its third digit.

B has a first digit that is one more than its second digit, and a second digit that is one more than its third digit.

C has a third digit that is equal to the sum of its first two digits.

D is an even number.

E is an odd number.

F is equal to three times number A.

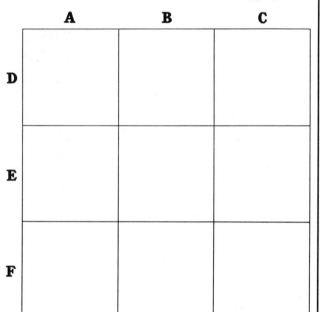

PUZZLE BY PETER GORDON

Out on a Limb

There are 18 trees hiding in the sentences below. Each one reads from left to right, across one or more words. The first tree, REDWOOD, is underlined for you. Can you spot the rest?

Answers, page 172

1. We sca<u>red wood</u>peckers as we raced around Nashville Monday morning.

2. The cloak and cap pleased my pal Mel mildly.

3. The silo customarily is calm on days when the corn is thick or yellow.

4. The map leads you to the real archway, which has pentagonal designs.

5. Since in school I've given them lockers, the students will owe me spruced-up hallways.

Magic Hex

This design is made up of seven hexagons (six-sided shapes) that share some edges with each other. Can you fill in each of the empty circles with a one-digit number so that the six numbers around every hexagon add up to exactly 30?

Answer, page 172

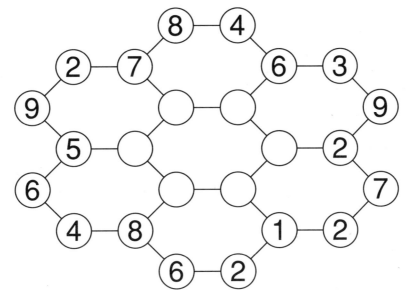

Categories

This puzzle is based on the old game of Categories. In each box, write the name of something that fits the category described at the left, and that also begins with the letter at the top. We've filled in an example to help get you started.

Answers, page 172

	C	L	A	S	H
Things relating to Valentine's Day	CARDS				
Units of measure					
Drinks					
Occupations					
Words containing the letter "Z"					

Play by Number

Find the value of each of the 20 letters below. Next, in the boxes at the bottom of the page, write these letters in order from lowest to highest value. Finally, find the longest word that can be read (from left to right, in consecutive boxes) within the row of 20 letters.

Answers, page 172

A = Volume, in cubic feet, of a cube whose edge is four feet long

B = The only number that does not change no matter what you multiply it by

C = The only even prime number

D = Area of this rectangle in square meters

5 meters
7 meters

E = When you multiply 12,345,679 × 9, the number of digits in the answer that are 1s

F = Remainder of 25,497 ÷ 1,413

G = 60% of 240

H = Number of inches in 20.32 centimeters

I = $\frac{17}{8} \div \frac{4}{13}$

J = 25.24 + 78.31 − 67.97, rounded off to the nearest tens' place

K = π, to the nearest hundredths' place

L = Fraction of the time that a "4" will come up when a regular six-sided die is rolled

M = 1.91 × 3.572

N = Degrees in a right angle

O = The fractional part of $\frac{713}{10}$ when it is written as a mixed number

P = Sum of the numbers 1 to 17 inclusive

Q = A googol

R = Number of sides on a dodecagon

S = (7 − 4) × (14 ÷ 7)

T = Average of 6,003, −4,123,   209, −1,492, and −559

Now, write the letters in order from lowest to highest.

The longest word that can be found consecutively in this sequence of 20 letters is _____.

Stately Names

This is a good puzzle to do with your family or friends. The shaded states on this map, as well as the state capitals marked with a star, all have something in common. Each of their names contains a familiar first name. For example, the name ANN can be found in **ANN**APOLIS (the capital of Maryland), and ART can be found in H**ART**FORD (the capital of Connecticut).

Can you think of the states or state capitals whose names contain the other first names below? Write each place's name on the blank space, then locate it on the map and write the number of that name in the correct circle. (We've done this for the first two to get you started.) Three of the names can be found in more than one place, and one of the states contains two different names.

Answers, page 172

First Name / **State or State Capital**

1. ANN — *Annapolis*
2. ART — *Hartford*
3. CAROL _____
   _____
4. CHARLES _____
5. DIANA _____
   _____
6. EVA _____
7. FLO _____
8. FRANK _____
9. GUS _____
10. HELEN _____
11. IDA _____
    _____
12. JACK _____
13. JEFF _____
14. JUNE _____
15. KEN _____
16. LOUIS _____
17. LULU _____
18. MARY _____
19. PAUL _____
20. PIA _____
21. RICH _____
22. SAL _____
23. TEX _____
24. TRENT _____
25. VAN _____
26. WES _____

G A M E S

Three-Sum

How many triangles in the large triangle below contain dots adding up to a multiple of three (3, 6, 9, 12, etc.)? Be careful! The triangles may be upside down and of any size.

Answers, page 173

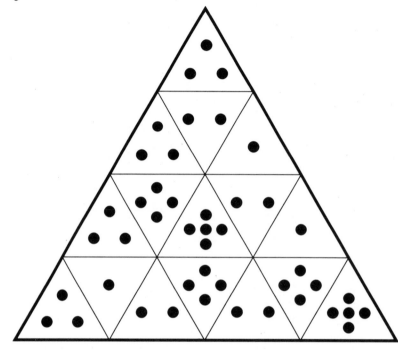

PUZZLE BY PETER GORDON

Break It Up

To complete each sentence, fill in the longest blank with a word that can be broken up to form two new words that fit, in order, in the short blanks. How many can you solve? Example: How OFTEN can you guess one OF TEN cards that I am holding in my hand?

Answers, page 173

1. The 150-page story about the fire-breathing _____ seemed to _____ _____.

2. Meet _____ _____ the _____ counter so that we can pick out the steaks for dinner.

3. Ma and _____ _____ a small apartment since they don't have to _____ us anymore.

4. As we were wheeling the shopping _____ _____ the lumpy pavement, a milk _____ fell out.

5. Susan will be angry because that _____ _____ _____ before you put your dirty clothes in it!

6. An _____ , such as Hawaii, _____ _____ that is completely surrounded by water.

PUZZLE BY KAREN ANDERSON

G A M E S

Facts and Figures

This quiz will test your trivia knowledge and research skills, as well as a bit of your mathematical ability. Answer the 13 questions below, and write the answers on the blanks next to the questions. Each of the answers will be a number. After you have filled in all the blanks, add up all the numbers and write the total in the box at the bottom.

Answers, page 173

1. ___ How many months are in a decade?

2. ___ How many baseball teams are in the National League?

3. ___ How many colors are on the flag of France?

4. ___ How many times does the word "ONE" appear on a dollar bill?

5. ___ How many South American countries do not border on the ocean?

6. ___ How many members of the House of Representatives represent Kansas?

7. ___ What is the country telephone dialing code for Ireland?

8. ___ What is the total number of eyes pictured on all the kings, queens, and jacks of a standard deck of cards?

9. ___ How many faces does an icosahedron have?

10. ___ How many different properties can be bought in a Monopoly game?

11. ___ What number of years was mentioned at the start of Lincoln's Gettysburg Address?

12. ___ What number is *acht* in German, *huit* in French, and *ocho* in Spanish?

13. ___ In the United States, how many states have more than one word in their names?

TOTAL _____

Seven Up!

These seven teasers actually form one big puzzle. Each small puzzle has a single letter as its solution. If you answer each one correctly and put the letters in order from one to seven, you will spell a word. *Answers, page 173*

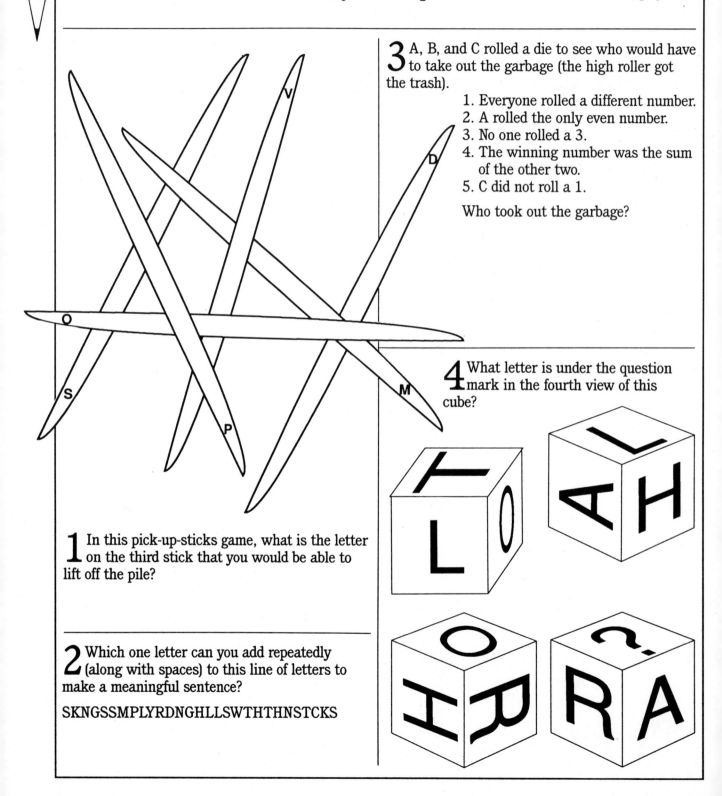

3 A, B, and C rolled a die to see who would have to take out the garbage (the high roller got the trash).

1. Everyone rolled a different number.
2. A rolled the only even number.
3. No one rolled a 3.
4. The winning number was the sum of the other two.
5. C did not roll a 1.

Who took out the garbage?

4 What letter is under the question mark in the fourth view of this cube?

1 In this pick-up-sticks game, what is the letter on the third stick that you would be able to lift off the pile?

2 Which one letter can you add repeatedly (along with spaces) to this line of letters to make a meaningful sentence?

SKNGSSMPLYRDNGHLLSWTHTHNSTCKS

5 After you solve this crossword, find the one letter that can go in the center square to form nine-letter words reading across and down.

ACROSS

1 Room for a sheik's wives
6 Taxi
9 Dwelling place
10 Ginger __ (soft drink)
11 Negative item on an accounting sheet
12 102, in Roman numerals
13 All whipped up, as eggs
15 Nerve
18 __-pong (table tennis)
19 Stick (to)
21 Money put away for retirement: Abbr.
22 Spitting __ (exact likeness)
26 Opposite of yeses
27 Narrow to a point
28 Health resort
29 Use a door marked "in"

DOWN

1 Possessed
2 Honest __ (Lincoln)
3 Burglarize
4 Fit for eating
5 Measure (out)
6 Prickly desert plants
7 Creature from outer space
8 Human __ (person)
14 Tarzan, the __: 2 words
15 Makes progress
16 __ in the bucket (insignificant amount): 2 words
17 __ apso (small terrier)
20 Religious ceremony
23 Likely
24 __-whiz!
25 Make a boo-boo

6 Color in the shapes with dots in them to reveal a letter. The letter may be upper or lower case, and turned in any direction.

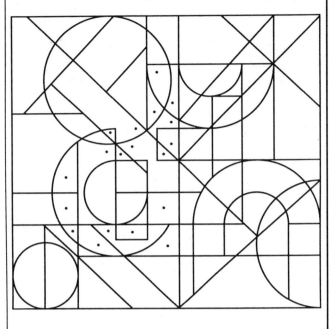

7 Answer the clues and put the answers on the numbered dashes. Then, fill in the blanks below the clues, transferring each letter to the blank above its number, to discover a sentence that will reveal the answer letter.

1. The highest temperature

$\overline{28}\ \overline{20}\ \overline{32}\ \overline{16}\ \overline{24}\ \overline{13}\ \overline{8}$

2. Excess $\underline{}\ \underline{}\ \underline{}\ \underline{}\ \underline{}$
$\quad\quad\ \ \overline{31}\ \overline{6}\ \overline{1}\ \overline{19}\ \overline{25}$

3. Dr. Seuss's *Butter __ Book*

$\overline{30}\ \overline{11}\ \overline{17}\ \overline{22}\ \overline{26}\ \overline{5}$

4. Incisors and molars $\underline{}\ \underline{}\ \underline{}\ \underline{}\ \underline{}$
$\quad\quad\quad\quad\quad\quad\quad\ \overline{7}\ \overline{15}\ \overline{3}\ \overline{12}\ \overline{23}$

5. Autumn $\underline{}\ \underline{}\ \underline{}\ \underline{}$
$\quad\quad\quad\ \overline{21}\ \overline{29}\ \overline{10}\ \overline{14}$

6. It can be touch-tone or rotary

$\overline{27}\ \overline{2}\ \overline{9}\ \overline{4}\ \overline{18}$

$\overline{1}\ \overline{2}\ \overline{3}\ \ \overline{4}\ \overline{5}\ \overline{6}\ \overline{7}\ \ \overline{8}\ \overline{9}$

$\overline{10}\ \overline{11}\ \overline{12}\ \overline{13}\ \ \overline{14}\ \overline{15}\ \overline{16}\ \overline{17}\ \overline{18}\ \overline{19}\ \ \overline{20}\ \overline{21}$

$\overline{22}\ \overline{23}\ \overline{24}\ \ \overline{25}\ \overline{26}\ \overline{27}\ \overline{28}\ \overline{29}\ \overline{30}\ \overline{31}\ \overline{32}$

Final answer:

6

All the Answers

1

10 SOUNDING OFF

1. KAPWEEEE! BLIP! BLIP! ZZAP!
2. KTCH SPSSSSH!
3. CRINCH CRUNCH CRINCH
4. dzzzt! dzzzt! dzzzt!
5. SPLAT!
6. AAKTSHOO!!
7. BIPPITA BOPPITA BIPPITA BOPPITA
8. GLUGG GLUGG GLUGG
9. SPLOOSH!

11 MATCH-UP 1

Music groups B and F are alike. The places where the others are different are circled below.

12 CONNECT-THE-DOTS 1

13 HIDE AND PEEK

1. Four kids were hiding.
2. Junior was holding a cookie from the plate on the table.
3. There were two giraffes on the mantelpiece.
4. Tennis and baseball (or softball)
5. A pair of slippers
6.

14 EYEBALL BENDERS

1. Water pistol
2. Domino
3. Jacks
4. Cabbage Patch doll
5. Checker on checkerboard

15 MATCH-UP 2

Gremlins C and E are exactly alike.

16 CHAIR AND CHAIR ALIKE

1. B (director, director's chair)
2. F (baby, high chair)
3. D (moviegoer, theater seat)
4. C (woman with new hairdo, beauty parlor seat)
5. I (airline passenger, airplane seat)
6. G (old woman, rocking chair)
7. A (king, throne)
8. H (student, school chair)
9. J (man drinking ice cream soda, ice cream parlor bar stool)
10. E (lifeguard, lifeguard's chair)

18 TRIANGLE TANGLE 1

19 HIGHWAY MAZE

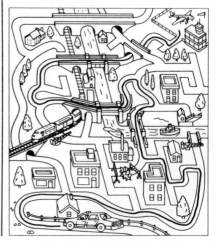

20 S IS FOR SATURDAY

We found 44 things beginning with S in the picture. How about you?

Sailboat, sailor, sandal, sandwich, scarf, scout, see-saw, Seven-up, sheriff, shirts, shoes, shorts, shoulders, skateboard, skates, skis, sky, skyline (and skyscrapers), smiles, snail, sneakers, soccer ball, socks, soda, soldier, sombrero, spoon, spot (on dog), squirrel, stairs, star, statue, steps, stickers (on suitcase), straw, strings (on guitar), stripe (on shirt), stroller, suitcase, sun, sunglasses, suspenders, swings, sword.

21 MIXTURE PICTURES

1. dart cart
2. bear chair
3. car jar
4. corn horn
5. bread bed
6. tail pail
7. hose nose
8. snail scale
9. lamp stamp

23 JUNGLE QUEST

22 CONNECT-THE-DOTS 2

26 F IS FOR FARM

We found 48 things beginning with F in the picture. How about you?

Faces, falcon (on weathervane), family, fan, farm, farmer, father, faucet, fawn, feather, fence, fender, fern, fields, fin (on fish), fingers, fire, fir trees, fish, fisherman, fist, five (on mailbox), flag, flame, flashlight, flowers, flies, foal, food, foot, football, Ford, forelegs, forehead, forest, fork, forklift, fox, frame, frankfurter, Franklin stove, freezer, fringe (on jacket), Frisbee, frog, fruit, fur (on animals), furniture.

24 HATS OFF!

The correct matches are as follows: A-6 (fireman, farmer); B-8 (clown, nurse); C-5 (baseball player, miner); D-7 (graduate, lumberjack); E-4 (chef, snake charmer); F-2 (sailor, magician); G-1 (astronaut, cowboy); H-3 (king, boy).

27 TRIANGLE TANGLE 2

28 WHAT'S WRONG? 1

We found 14 errors:
1. Two trees are growing together.
2. There is a snowplow shovel on the golf cart.
3. There is a traffic light on the course.
4. The man is swinging with two clubs.
5. There is a miniature golf windmill on the green.
6. The tee and the green for the 13th hole are next to each other.
7. The man's reflection in the pond is backward.
8. There is a diving board by the pond.
9. There is a pail and shovel in the sand trap.
10. The footprints in the sand trap are too large.
11. The woman is hitting a bowling ball.
12. There is a 19th hole.
13. The man is putting with a baseball bat.
14. A squirrel is golfing.

29 CONNECT-THE-DOTS 3

In order, the pictures are: apple, baseball, camel, die, elephant, frog, giraffe, hat, igloo, judge, kangaroo, leaf, magician, note, octopus, pencil, queen, robot, scissors, turtle, umbrella, vest, watch, xylophone, yo-yo, and zebra.

31 BACK TO SCHOOL

30 MATCH-UP 3

B and E are exactly alike.

32 J IS FOR JUNIOR'S ROOM

We found 28 items beginning with J in the picture. How about you?

Jacks, jacket, jack-in-the-box, jackknife, jack-o-lantern, jack rabbit, January, Japan, jar, javelin, *Jaws* (the movie on TV), jeans, jeep, jelly beans, jellyfish, jet, jewelry, jigsaw puzzle, jockey, joke book, joker, Jolly Roger, joy stick, jug, juice, jukebox, jump rope, Junior himself (who is a juvenile and has a jaw, if you want to be very complete).

33 MIDNIGHT MUNCHIES

The yogurt, gouda cheese, salami, grapes, chicken, orange, and raisins are in the refrigerator. The apple juice, bagel, and banana are not.

34 HEY DIDDLE RIDDLE

Why does a hen lay an egg? Because she can't lay a brick.

35 WHAT'S WRONG? 2

We found 11 errors:
1. The hammock is attached to a tree that is too far away.
2. The bird feeder is coin-operated.
3. The chef's apron says "St. Louis Yankees" (the Yankees are in New York).
4. The chef is using a shovel on the grill.
5. The badminton net is a spider's web.
6. The girl is using a fly swatter as a racket.
7. The suntan lotion is labeled "cooking oil."

8. The boy has on a shirt with one long sleeve and one short one.
9. The title of the woman's book is written as a mirror image.
10. There is no back support on the lounge chair.
11. The front right table leg goes behind the bar connecting the left and right legs.

36 HEADS OR TAILS?

1-E, rooster; 2-A, alligator; 3-D, beaver; 4-J, pig; 5-F, lobster; 6-I, walrus; 7-H, rabbit; 8-B, poodle; 9-C, raccoon; 10-G, lizard.

38 TRICK-OR-TREAT MAZE

39 P IS FOR PET SHOP

We found 35 things beginning with P in the picture. How about you?

Pad (of paper), paddle, pail, palm trees, panda, pants, paperweight, parachute, parents, parka, parrot, party hat, paw prints, peanuts, pear, pearl, pebbles (at bottoms of aquariums), pencil, penguin, perch, pirate ship, piggy bank, plaid (hat), plants (in tanks), polka dots (on boy's shirt), pompom (on panda's hat), ponytail, poodle, popsicle, poster, price tag, puppies, purse (or pocketbook), pussycat, pyramid.

40 CLASSROOM CAPER

We found 13 errors:
1. The addition on the blackboard is incorrect.
2. The United States map is upside down.
3. The teacher is pointing with an umbrella.
4. The S and the T in the alphabet banner are reversed.
5. The clock has two minute hands.
6. The teacher's chair has only three legs.
7. The boy at the front of the room is sharpening a pen.
8. The teacher is wearing two different types of shoes.
9. The desk in the middle of the front row has a table setting on it.
10. The desk on the right in the front row has an animal foot as a leg.
11. The boy on the left in the back row is facing the wrong way.
12. The middle desk in the back row has a phone on it.
13. The book on the desk at the right in the back row opens the wrong way.

42 CONNECT-THE-DOTS 4

41 NATURE'S SECRETS

44 C IS FOR CIRCUS

We found 39 things beginning with C in the picture. How about you?

Calliope, camel, can, cannon, cannonballs, canopy, cape, car, carrot, cartwheel, cat, chair, checkers (on clown costume), chimpanzees, chins, cigar, circles (on cushion), circus, cloak, clowns, clouds (of dust), coat, collar, collie, colt, concession stand (the snack bar), cone (on clown's hat), confetti, cord, costume, cotton candy, cowboy, crank (on car), cream pie, crepe paper, riding crop, crowd, crown, and cushions.

46 CHRISTMAS MAZE

47 TRIANGLE TANGLE 3

43 WHAT'S WRONG? 3

We found 16 errors:
1. The rope from the tire is not attached to the tree.
2. Two different types of fruit are growing on the tree.
3. The tent has a chimney.
4. The tent has a glass window.
5. One mountain, between two others with snow caps, does not have snow at its peak.
6. A pencil is being used as a tent stake.
7. The bear has sunglasses on.
8. The water pump has a shower head.
9. There is a manhole cover on the ground.
10. The boy on the bench has a pot on his head.
11. The bench is missing a leg (where the boy is sitting).
12. The toaster is electric, and not plugged in.
13. The flame in the lamp is upside down.
14. The boy by the fire is toasting a baseball.
15. The boy by the fire is wearing winter clothes.
16. A bird is coming out of a hole in the ground.

G
A
M
E
S

45 CABIN HIDEAWAY

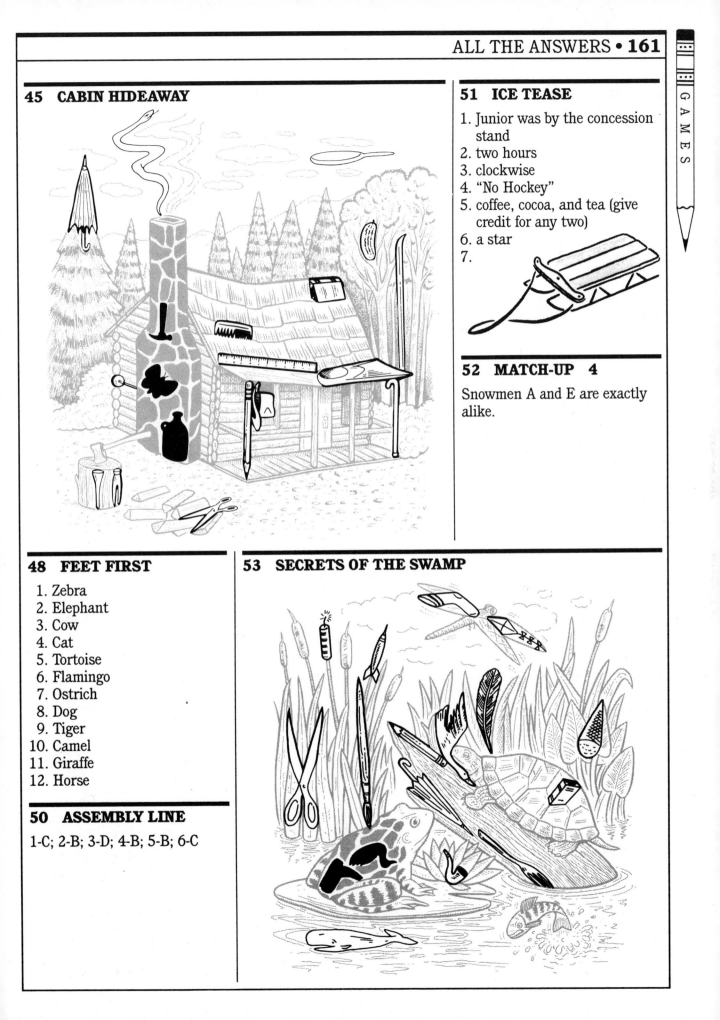

51 ICE TEASE

1. Junior was by the concession stand
2. two hours
3. clockwise
4. "No Hockey"
5. coffee, cocoa, and tea (give credit for any two)
6. a star
7.

52 MATCH-UP 4

Snowmen A and E are exactly alike.

48 FEET FIRST

1. Zebra
2. Elephant
3. Cow
4. Cat
5. Tortoise
6. Flamingo
7. Ostrich
8. Dog
9. Tiger
10. Camel
11. Giraffe
12. Horse

50 ASSEMBLY LINE

1-C; 2-B; 3-D; 4-B; 5-B; 6-C

53 SECRETS OF THE SWAMP

54 STRANGE HAPPENINGS

1. H (fruit bowl)
2. G (nail file)
3. B (ski jump)
4. E (picket fence)
5. C (comic strip)
6. D (square dance)
7. F (home run)
8. I (hat box)
9. A (bell hop)

56 WHOSE HUES?

When you are done coloring, you should see a parrot.

2

58 PICTURE CROSSWORD 1

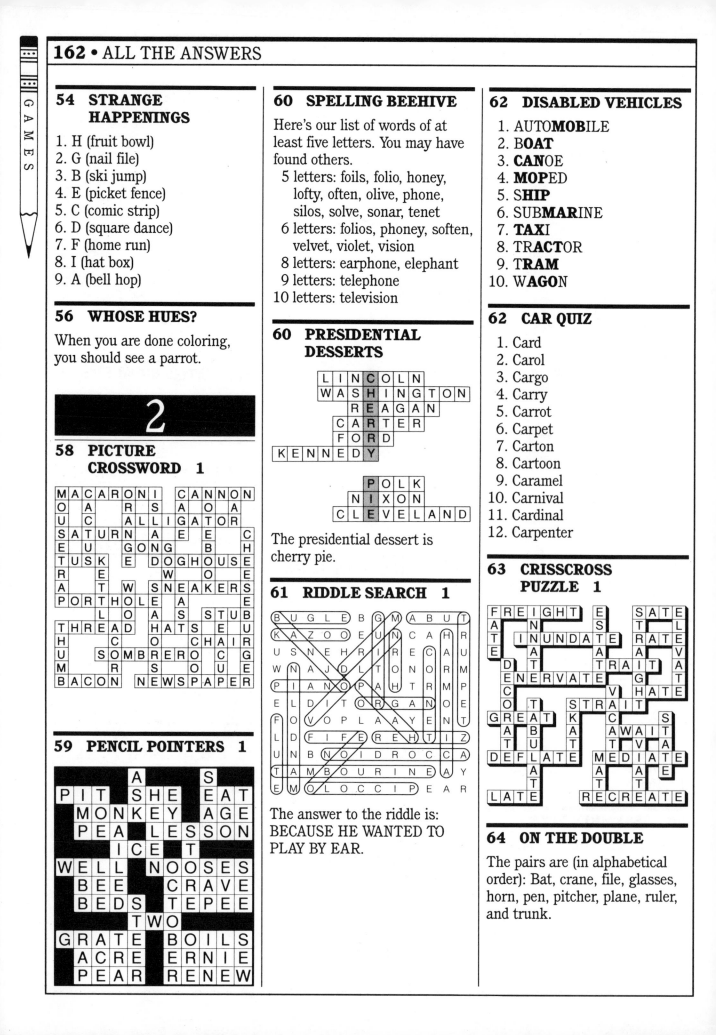

59 PENCIL POINTERS 1

60 SPELLING BEEHIVE

Here's our list of words of at least five letters. You may have found others.

5 letters: foils, folio, honey, lofty, often, olive, phone, silos, solve, sonar, tenet

6 letters: folios, phoney, soften, velvet, violet, vision

8 letters: earphone, elephant

9 letters: telephone

10 letters: television

60 PRESIDENTIAL DESSERTS

The presidential dessert is cherry pie.

61 RIDDLE SEARCH 1

The answer to the riddle is: BECAUSE HE WANTED TO PLAY BY EAR.

62 DISABLED VEHICLES

1. AUTO**MOB**ILE
2. B**OAT**
3. **CAN**OE
4. **MOP**ED
5. S**HIP**
6. SUB**MAR**INE
7. **TAX**I
8. TRA**CT**OR
9. T**RAM**
10. W**AGO**N

62 CAR QUIZ

1. Card
2. Carol
3. Cargo
4. Carry
5. Carrot
6. Carpet
7. Carton
8. Cartoon
9. Caramel
10. Carnival
11. Cardinal
12. Carpenter

63 CRISSCROSS PUZZLE 1

64 ON THE DOUBLE

The pairs are (in alphabetical order): Bat, crane, file, glasses, horn, pen, pitcher, plane, ruler, and trunk.

GAMES

65 CROSSWORD PUZZLE 1

B	I	T		R	A	T		A	N	D	S
A	C	E		E	I	O		T	O	R	A	H
D	E	E	R	F	L	Y		S	T	A	L	E
		T	I	S	S	U	E		G	E	M
L	A	B	E	L			T	A	C	O
E	M	U		E	A	S	T		I	N	C	H
N	E	T	S		L	I	E		A	F	R	O
A	N	T	I		A	P	R	S		L	A	P
	E	X	A	M		T	H	Y	M	E
E	R	R		B	O	O	B	O	O
D	A	F	F	Y		F	I	R	E	F	L	Y
S	I	L	O	S		I	K	E		R	O	E
	D	Y	E	S		T	E	D		I	T	S

66 FROM HOUSE TO HOUSE

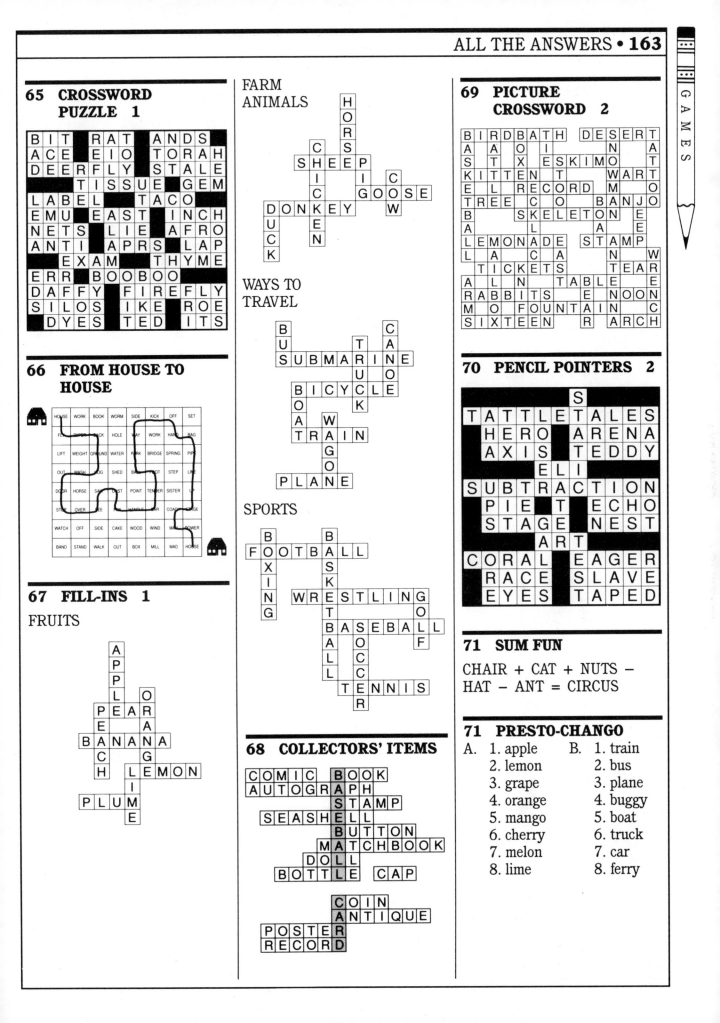

67 FILL-INS 1

FRUITS

APPLE
PEAR
ORANGE
BANANA
PEACH
LEMON
LIME
PLUM

FARM ANIMALS

HORSE · CHICKEN · SHEEP · PIG · GOOSE · COW · DONKEY · DUCK · HEN

WAYS TO TRAVEL

BUS · CANOE · SUBMARINE · TRUCK · BICYCLE · BOAT · WAGON · TRAIN · PLANE

SPORTS

BOXING · BASKETBALL · FOOTBALL · WRESTLING · GOLF · BASEBALL · SOCCER · TENNIS

68 COLLECTORS' ITEMS

COMIC · BOOK · AUTOGRAPH · STAMP · SEASHELL · BUTTON · MATCHBOOK · DOLL · BOTTLE · CAP · COIN · ANTIQUE · POSTER · RECORD

69 PICTURE CROSSWORD 2

BIRDBATH · DESERT · ASK · KITTEN · ESKIMO · WART · TREE · RECORD · BANJO · SKELETON · LEMONADE · STAMP · TICKETS · TEAR · TABLE · NOON · RABBITS · FOUNTAIN · SIXTEEN · ARCH

70 PENCIL POINTERS 2

T	A	T	T	L	E	T	A	L	E	S
	H	E	R	O		A	R	E	N	A
	A	X	I	S		T	E	D	D	Y
			E	L	I	
S	U	B	T	R	A	C	T	I	O	N
P	I	E		T		E	C	H	O
S	T	A	G	E		N	E	S	T
		A	R	T	
C	O	R	A	L		E	A	G	E	R
R	A	C	E		S	L	A	V	E
E	Y	E	S		T	A	P	E	D

(S above SUBTRACTION column)

71 SUM FUN

CHAIR + CAT + NUTS − HAT − ANT = CIRCUS

71 PRESTO-CHANGO

A. 1. apple
2. lemon
3. grape
4. orange
5. mango
6. cherry
7. melon
8. lime

B. 1. train
2. bus
3. plane
4. buggy
5. boat
6. truck
7. car
8. ferry

72 PET REBUSES

1. CANE + BAT − BEAN = CAT
2. DOLL + BAG − BALL = DOG
3. FIST + SHOE − TOES = FISH
4. HOSE + CAR − ACES + SLIDE − LID = HORSE
5. HAIR + BANK − RAIN + MONSTER − KNOB = HAMSTER

73 CROSSWORD PUZZLE 2

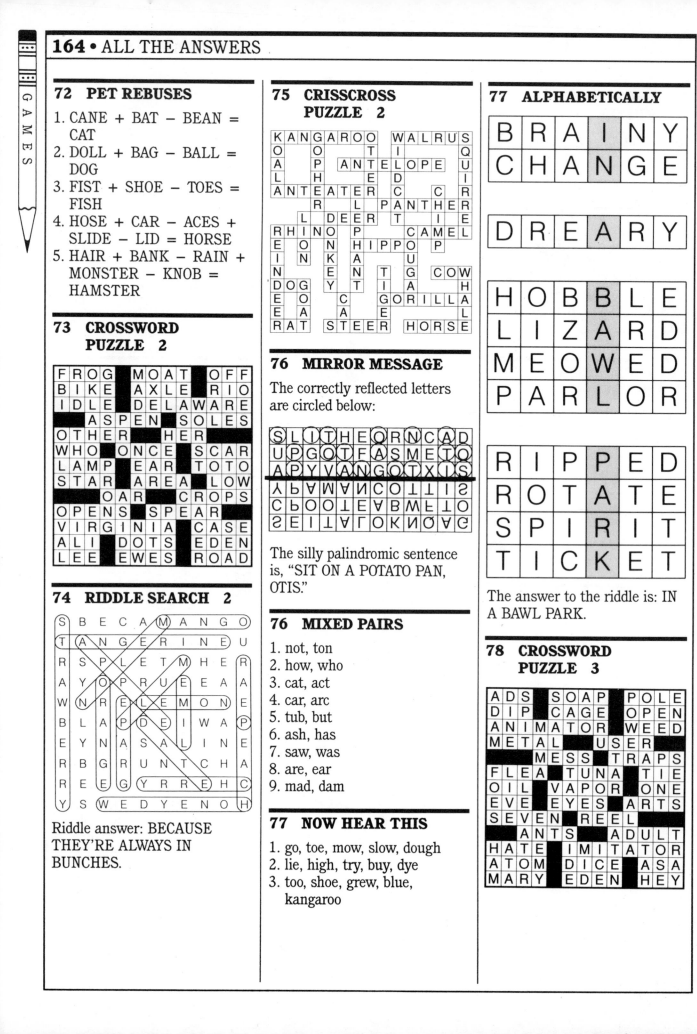

74 RIDDLE SEARCH 2

Riddle answer: BECAUSE THEY'RE ALWAYS IN BUNCHES.

75 CRISSCROSS PUZZLE 2

76 MIRROR MESSAGE

The correctly reflected letters are circled below:

The silly palindromic sentence is, "SIT ON A POTATO PAN, OTIS."

76 MIXED PAIRS

1. not, ton
2. how, who
3. cat, act
4. car, arc
5. tub, but
6. ash, has
7. saw, was
8. are, ear
9. mad, dam

77 NOW HEAR THIS

1. go, toe, mow, slow, dough
2. lie, high, try, buy, dye
3. too, shoe, grew, blue, kangaroo

77 ALPHABETICALLY

The answer to the riddle is: IN A BAWL PARK.

78 CROSSWORD PUZZLE 3

79 BODY BUILDING

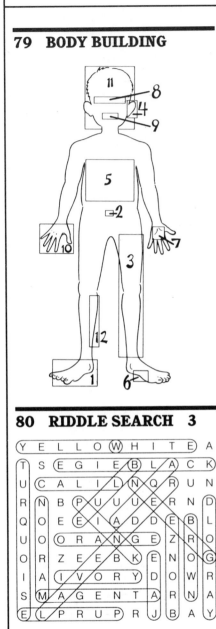

80 RIDDLE SEARCH 3

The answer to the riddle is: A
SUNBURNED ZEBRA

81 PICTURE CROSSWORD 3

```
J A C K S   B A S E B A L L
O       I   U   A   P   O   I
Y A R N   S T   D E E R   O   G
S       G I A N T   D   L   H
T E A   N   O   L   K N O T   T
I   M   D O N K E Y   A   N
C   B   A       A   I
K N U C K L E S   W A G O N
L   A   H O R N   A   T
T R A I N   O   A   T
H   N G   E   T I G E R S
R E C T A N G L E   R   N
E   E   R   A   A L A S K A
A   O   C A N   D   K
D O G H O U S E   T W E L V E
```

82 CROSSWORD PUZZLE 4

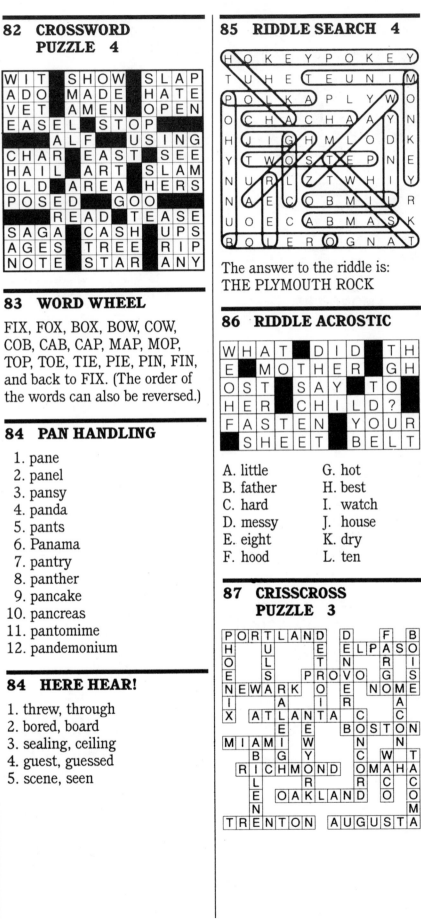

83 WORD WHEEL

FIX, FOX, BOX, BOW, COW, COB, CAB, CAP, MAP, MOP, TOP, TOE, TIE, PIE, PIN, FIN, and back to FIX. (The order of the words can also be reversed.)

84 PAN HANDLING

1. pane
2. panel
3. pansy
4. panda
5. pants
6. Panama
7. pantry
8. panther
9. pancake
10. pancreas
11. pantomime
12. pandemonium

84 HERE HEAR!

1. threw, through
2. bored, board
3. sealing, ceiling
4. guest, guessed
5. scene, seen

85 RIDDLE SEARCH 4

The answer to the riddle is:
THE PLYMOUTH ROCK

86 RIDDLE ACROSTIC

```
W H A T   D I D   T H
E M O T H E R   G H
O S T   S A Y   T O
H E R   C H I L D ?
F A S T E N   Y O U R
  S H E E T   B E L T
```

A. little   G. hot
B. father   H. best
C. hard   I. watch
D. messy   J. house
E. eight   K. dry
F. hood   L. ten

87 CRISSCROSS PUZZLE 3

88 PENCIL POINTERS 3

89 AMONG THE FLOWERS

1. day
2. vet
3. mile
4. owl
5. maid
6. pony
7. May
8. hiss
9. bull
10. comb
11. older
12. hint
13. snoop
14. pint
15. carton
16. apron
17. anthem

90 RIDDLE SEARCH 5

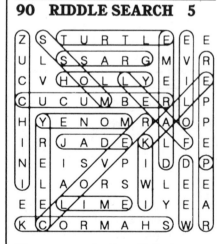

The answer to the riddle is: ELVIS PARSLEY.

91 PUZZLING FILL-INS

1. buzz
2. fizz
3. jazz
4. pizza
5. dizzy
6. fuzzy
7. frizzy
8. nozzle
9. sizzle
10. muzzle
11. buzzard
12. drizzle
13. swizzle
14. grizzly
15. blizzard

91 BUMPER CROP

The name reading down the columns is flower garden.

92 BUILD-A-WORD

The new words are: pantry, pepper, gotten, carrot, mildew, notice, sacred, canyon, rather, and cotton.

92 HORSING AROUND

The bonus horse is Pegasus, the winged horse of Greek mythology.

93 CROSSWORD PUZZLE 5

ZAP FARM JOKE
ORE OBOE AWES
NET NEON PENS
EASED TUBA
YAM UNDER
WADE AGES ARE
HUES TAX IRAN
ATE DELI REST
TORSO TEA
LESS SQUAD
CASE KITS SLY
ACHE IDEA EVE
BEEP DENY DAD

94 PROVERBIAL CONFUSION

Pair #1
It's never too late to learn.
You can't teach an old dog new tricks.

Pair #2
Seek and you shall find.
Curiosity killed the cat.

Pair #3
Two heads are better than one.
Too many cooks spoil the broth.

94 FILL-INS 2

1. bark
2. barn
3. barge
4. barber
5. barley
6. barrel
7. Barbie
8. barrier
9. bargain
10. barrette
11. barracuda
12. barometer

95 RIDDLEGRAMS

1. A) Line B) Deer C) Vote D) Card
The answer to the riddle is: CINDERELEVATOR.
2. A) Bag B) Train C) Rip D) Near
The answer to the riddle is: GRAPE BRITAIN.

96 SEEING THINGS

1. Bulldog
2. Earthworm
3. Catfish
4. Funny bone
5. Cupcake
6. Butterfly
7. Firecrackers
8. Goldfish

98 DINOSAUR QUIZ

1. a
2. c
3. c
4. False (Stegosaurs became extinct millions of years before tyrannosaurs lived.)
5. False

6. False (A stegosaur's brain was about the size of a walnut.)

7. True

8. *Borosaurus* is the fake.

Note: Dinosaur names, with some exceptions, can appear in two different ways—either capitalized, with a final-us, or uncapitalized, without the -us. The name with the -us is the name of the dinosaur's "genus," which is a type of classification that can include more than one similar species. Genus names usually appear in italics. It is therefore correct to say, for example, that a stegosaur is a dinosaur belonging to the genus *Stegosaurus*.

99 DINOSAUR EYEBALL BENDERS

a. plesiosaur
b. apatosaur (formerly known as a brontosaur)
c. tyrannosaur
d. stegosaur
e. saber-toothed tiger
f. woolly mammoth
g. triceratops
h. pterodactyl

The woolly mammoth and saber-toothed tiger were mammals. Plesiosaurs, which lived in the water, and pterodactyls, which could fly, were both reptiles, but are not classified as dinosaurs. The rest are true dinosaurs.

100 RIDDLE ME THIS

1-E, 2-D (rust "eats" iron), 3-B, 4-G, 5-A, 6-C, 7-H, 8-F.
Adapted from *263 Brain Busters*, by Louis Phillips, © Louis Phillips, 1985. Used by arrangement with Viking, Penguin, Inc.

102 THE OLDEN DAZE

1. C	5. C	9. B
2. C	6. B	10. A
3. A	7. A	11. B
4. A	8. C	12. C

104 CAN YOU GUESS

1. 206
2. 2½ ounces
3. 5 feet
4. 1,050
5. $600
6. more than 30,000

105 PLAY BALL!

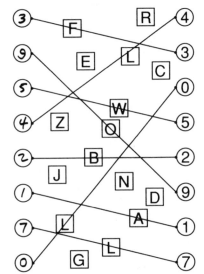

Riddle answer: BECAUSE THEY HEARD THERE WOULD BE A FOWL BALL!

106 WHICH CAME FIRST?

1. The first night baseball game was played first, on June 2, 1883, in Fort Wayne, Indiana. The first night football game was played in 1892 at the Mansfield Fair, in Mansfield, Pennsylvania.

2. The safety pin was invented first, in 1849, by Walter Hunt. The golf tee was invented in 1899 by George F. Grant of Boston, Massachusetts.

3. Potato chips came before chop suey. The first ones were cooked in a Saratoga Springs, New York, hotel in 1865, and were originally called Saratoga chips. Chop suey was not invented in China. It was, in fact, first cooked in New York City on August 29, 1896, for the Chinese Ambassador.

4. Basketball was invented in 1892 by James Naismith of Springfield, Massachusetts (where today's Basketball Hall of Fame is located). Three years later, not too far away in Holyoke, Massachusetts, George Morgan of the local YMCA developed the game of volleyball, which was originally called Mintonette.

5. Christmas cards came first. They were first engraved in 1875. The first long distance phone call—from Boston to New York City—was made on March 27, 1884.

6. These two events happened within a year of one another. The first reindeer to be born in the United States was in Beverly, Massachusetts, on May 31, 1929. A cow named Elm Farm Ollie was flown and milked in flight on February 18, 1930.

7. The stamp catalog came first. In 1862, U.S. postage stamps had been on the market for about 15 years, when the first postage stamp catalog made its appearance—*The Stamp Collector's Manual, Being a Complete Guide to the Collectors of American and Foreign Postage and Despatch Stamps.* The first automobile road map was published and distributed in 1914 by the Gulf Oil Company of Pittsburgh, Pennsylvania.

8. Men started wearing derby hats around 1850. Chester Greenwood of Farmington, Maine, invented earmuffs in 1873.

9. The pencil with attached eraser came first. We take it for granted that pencils have erasers on them, but pencils had been around for a while before Hyman L. Lipman patented the pencil with the attached eraser in 1858. In 1888, John J. Loud of Weymouth, Massachusetts, received a patent for his ball-point pen.

10. In 1892, William Painter obtained a patent for his invention—the bottle cap with cork in the crown. The first comic books (containing cartoons that had appeared in newspapers) were published in 1904.

11. Gertrude Ederle achieved international fame on August 6, 1926, when she became the first woman to swim the English Channel. The first airline stewardess was Ellen Church, for a United Airlines flight on May 15, 1930, between San Francisco, California, and Cheyenne, Wyoming.

12. The United States Congress authorized the minting of the first five-cent piece or "nickel" (even though the coin contained 75% copper and only 25% nickel) in 1866. The first parking meter made its appearance in Oklahoma City, in 1935.

108 ALASKA? I'LL ASK YA!

1. c (Ice fields cover about 4.9% of Alaska. If you're wondering about d, it's true because Alaska's Aleutian Islands cross the 180° longitude line,

which is where east meets west.)

2. a (along with Aleut)
3. d
4. c
5. True
6. d (Canadian igloos are made of ice.)
7. d
8. False (Anchorage has the highest cost of living of any city in the U.S.)
9. c

110 WHAT'S IN A GAME?

1. C (This is partly because of Illinois Avenue's location, and partly because there's a card that sends you there.)
   B
   A
   D (At the start of the game, you have $1,500. You have to pay either 10 percent of this, which is $150, or $200. Of course, you would choose to pay only $150.)

2. D (There are also boxed and computer versions of this game.)
   C
   B (It's the checker variation in which the object is to lose all your pieces. There are also "Giveaway" versions of chess.)
   A (Klondike is the name of the most common form of card solitaire. It's the game that starts with seven piles, and in which you can place a red 7 on a black 8, etc.)

3. C (In a common form of darts, a player must hit 301 exactly, and must begin and end the game by hitting a "double" space on the dartboard.)
   A (This is according to the *Guinness Book of World Records*.)
   B
   D (This is according to the *Guinness Book of World Records*.

The contest was held at the State University of New York at Albany. There were three players per mat, and winners were consolidated on new mats as players were eliminated.)

4. B (Draughts is the British name.)
   D (Noughts-and-crosses is the British name.)
   A (Pipopipette is the French name for this paper-and-pencil game of connecting dots to make boxes, but the name also appears in some English language books.)
   C (Reversi was the game's original name when it was invented in England in the 1880s. The name "Othello" is a trademark now owned by Hasbro/Milton Bradley, but other companies still put out the game under the name reversi.)

111 STATES OF CONFUSION

1. Indiana
2. Tennessee
3. Oklahoma
4. West Virginia
5. Texas
6. Nevada
7. New York
8. Hawaii
9. Montana
10. Washington
11. Maine
12. South Carolina
13. Louisiana
14. Delaware
15. Nebraska
16. Florida

112 WHO WAS IT?

1. B
2. B
3. B
4. B (Eli Whitney invented the cotton gin—a machine to separate the cotton seeds from the cotton.)
5. A
6. A
7. A (Gillette invented the safety razor.)
8. A
9. B
10. A
11. B (Celsius invented his version of a thermometer 28 years later, using his temperature scale.)
12. B
13. A (Howe invented the sewing machine.)
14. B

114 TWELVE TOUGH TEASERS

1. One of the ways the figure can be copied is shown by the arrows. It is necessary to begin and end with the ends of the long horizontal line, since drawing a line to one of these points puts you at a dead end.

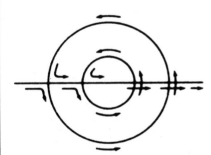

2. GAMES *Junior*, like all other modern magazines, has odd-numbered pages on the right. Therefore, pages 15 and 16 are the front and back of a single page, and nothing could have been found between them.

3. Two minutes. It takes one minute for the front of the train to get through the tunnel, and one more minute for the back of the train to get through the tunnel.

4. Yes. The day Kim's parents spoke to her about the picnic was the day before yesterday. Since it didn't rain the next day (which was yesterday), the picnic went on as planned (today).

5. Six (two red, two yellow, and two green)

6. Besides the half dollar, I have a quarter, four dimes, and four pennies.

7. No, because if the man's wife is a widow, the man is no longer alive!

8. Here's one possible solution. (Your solution may look like this one turned sideways or upside down.)

	X				
			X		
					X
X					
		X			
				X	

9. No, it's impossible, and there's a very clever way to prove it. Imagine that the grid is colored like a checkerboard. Now it's clear that no matter how you place a domino to cover the two squares, the two squares will have different colors. But since there are 18 dark squares and only 16 light squares, you'll be left with two dark squares to cover after you've placed 16 dominoes—and there's no way you can do it.

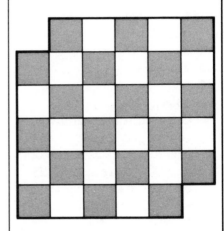

10. Minnesota

11. The trick is to make a three-dimensional figure (called a tetrahedron). One equilateral triangle, using three toothpicks, lies flat on the table. The other three toothpicks meet at a point above the triangle, and extend to the triangle's three corners. This forms three more triangles, as shown.

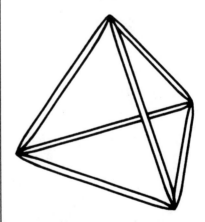

12. There is no missing dollar. The question is misleading, because there is no reason to add the $27 spent by the men and the $2 kept by the bellboy. Really, the $27 spent by the men is made up of the $25 spent for the room and the $2 kept by the bellboy.

116 CATS INCREDIBLE!

1. a-4, *kata*; b-7, *gato*; c-5, *katze*; d-6, *miu*; e-2, *qittah*; f-8, *koshka*; g-3, *chat*; h-1, *mao*.
2. c
3. True
4. e
5. False (There is no exact date, but it is generally accepted that the Egyptians first kept cats as pets 4,000 to 5,000 years ago. By the way, there is no year 0 on our calendar; 1 B.C. was followed by 1 A.D.)
6. False (Cats can see color, although not very well.)
7. d
8. True
9. d (Cats can see with much less light than humans, but they cannot see in total darkness.)
10. a-5; b-4; c-2; d-3; e-1.

118 WHAT'S THE DIFFERENCE?

Here are our answers. Other correct answers are possible.
1. The penny is a different color. The nickel is tail-side up. The dime is worth an even number of cents.
2. The lion has no stripes. The tiger is lying down (or, the tiger is a native of Asia instead of Africa). The zebra is not a feline.
3. Colorado has straight-line borders (or, Colorado is a state, not a country). Cuba is an island (or, Cuba ends with the letter A). Mexico begins with the letter M.
4. The record is by Michael Jackson. The price of the disc is $13. The cassette is not shaped like a disc (or, it's not in its package).
5. The canoe contains a girl. The raft is not made of wood (or, the person in the raft is facing a different direction). The rowboat has two oars rather than one paddle.

119 HIGH-LOW QUIZ

1. LOW. The typical price for a compact disc is $14.98.
2. HIGH. A Baby Ruth candy bar sold for 10¢ in 1952.
3. LOW. In 1982 you could have bought a complete set of Topps baseball cards for $21.
4. HIGH. In 1959 *MAD* sold for 25¢.
5. HIGH. In 1961 you could have bought wallet-sized photos of movie and TV stars for only 10¢.
6. LOW. The top price for an around-the-world cruise aboard the *QE2* in 1976 was $62,000 per person (double occupancy). There were, of course, cheaper cabins available.
7. LOW. In 1959 a four-blade Scout pocket knife sold for $1.50.
8. HIGH. In 1948 a six-bottle carton of Coke sold for 25¢ plus deposit. (Individual bottles cost a nickel.)

4

122 OUT OF ORDER 1

The correct order is: F, A, E, C, D, B.

124 DETECTIVE'S NOTEBOOK

Picture Mystery
Dumpty suddenly remembered that one of the items the shopper bought was a comb. The stranger couldn't have been the escaped criminal. Bart Hargrove was completely bald, and would have no reason to buy a comb. It seems that Dumpty did pay attention to appearances after all.

Lip Reading
1. E
2. A
3. F
4. D
5. B
6. C

126 THE DATING GAME

The correct order of the pages is: F, B, E, A, D, C.

127 WORK BOXES

128 OUT OF ORDER 2

The correct order is: D, A, F, E, C, B.

129 TREASURE HUNT

The X containing the treasure is the one labeled H.

From clue 1, you can rule out points A and G.

From clue 2, you can eliminate C.

From clue 3, you can eliminate E and I, which have even numbers of Xs to their north but are on the big island.

From clue 4, you can eliminate D and J. The distance from I to J is the same as the distance from the pirate hut to the sunken ship, and the distance from D to E is even less.

You now know that the treasure must be buried at either B, F, or H. Of these, only H has buildings both to its north and its west.

131 WHAT COMES NEXT?

The pen (A) comes next. The name of each pictured item is a rhyme for its number (for example, one-*sun*, two-*shoe*, three-*key*, etc.).

132 DETECTIVE'S NOTEBOOK

Picture Mystery

The picture shows there were at least three restaurants on Maple Street. Officer Dumpty never told the twins which restaurant's food had been ruined. The only way Tim and Kim could have known it was Pulski's was if they had been there that morning. Once Officer Dumpty pointed this out, Tim and Kim admitted their guilt.

Pigpen Code

Key is in mailbox

135 OUT OF ORDER 3

The correct answer is: C, F, B, E, D, A.

136 COLOR SCHEMES

Here are our solutions. Other answers may be possible.

1

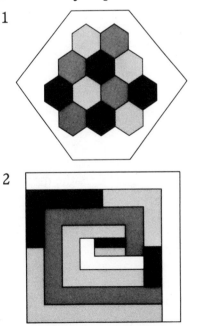

2

3

4

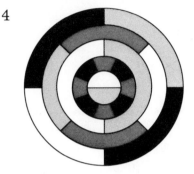

Incidentally, four colors are always enough to color a flat map according to the rule that touching areas must have different colors. Four colors are also enough for a map drawn on a sphere. But on some surfaces, a greater number of colors is needed. Some maps drawn on a surface shaped like a doughnut, for example, require as many as seven different colors.

137 LIGHTS OUT!

1-G; 2-H; 3-A; 4-D; 5-E; 6-F; 7-B; 8-C.

138 OUT OF ORDER 4

The correct order is: E, B, D, F, A, C.

139 TRIVIARITHMETIC

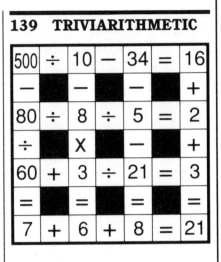

500	÷	10	−	34	=	16
−		−		−		+
80	÷	8	÷	5	=	2
÷		X		−		+
60	+	3	÷	21	=	3
=		=		=		=
7	+	6	+	8	=	21

141 SQUARE DEAL

The highest possible total is 31 (4 + 9 + 5 + 7 + 6), as shown.

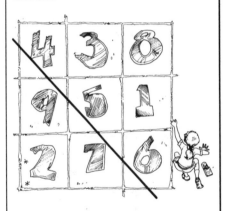

143 OUT OF ORDER 5

The correct order is: E, F, C, A, D, B.

144 LIZARD LOGIC

Felix was Amy's admirer. Since each neighbor told one lie, any boy who had both of or neither of the characteristic named by one neighbor can be eliminated. From the first neighbor, Boris, Calvin, and Dennis are disqualified. Abner, Calvin, Dennis, and Elmer are eliminated by neighbor two. The third neighbor rules out Abner, Boris, Calvin, Gomer, and Horace. That leaves only Felix.

5

146 CROSS NUMBERS

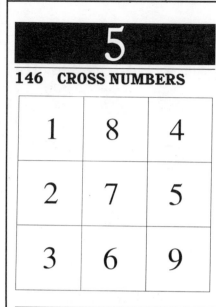

1	8	4
2	7	5
3	6	9

146 OUT ON A LIMB

1. Redwood, cedar, ash, lemon
2. Oak, apple, palm, elm
3. Locust, almond, hickory
4. Maple, larch, aspen
5. Olive, hemlock, willow, spruce

147 MAGIC HEX

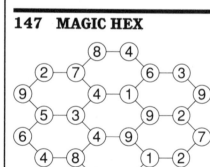

147 CATEGORIES

Our answers are as follows. (Other answers are also possible.)

Things relating to Valentine's Day: cards, love, arrows, sweets, hearts; **Units of measure:** carat, league, acre, second, hour; **Drinks:** coffee, lemonade, apple juice, soda, hot chocolate; **Occupations:** carpenter, lawyer, artist, salesman, hockey player; **Words containing the letter "Z":** crazy, lazy, amaze, size, hazy.

148 PLAY BY NUMBER

A = 64
B = 0
C = 2
D = 35
E = 9
F = 63
G = 144
H = 8
I = 6.90625
J = 40
K = 3.14
L = ¹⁄₁₆ or .166

M = 6.82252
N = 90
O = ³⁄₁₀ or .3
P = 153
Q = 10^{100}
R = 12
S = 6
T = 7.6

In order from lowest to highest: BLOCKSMITHERDJFANGPQ
The longest word: LOCKSMITH

149 STATELY NAMES

1. **ANN**APOLIS (Maryland)
2. H**ART**FORD (Connecticut)
3. NORTH **CAROL**INA; SOUTH **CAROL**INA
4. **CHARLES**TON (West Virginia)
5. IN**DIANA**; IN**DIANA**POLIS (Indiana)
6. N**EVA**DA
7. **FLO**RIDA
8. **FRANK**FORT (Kentucky)
9. AU**GUS**TA (Maine)
10. **HELEN**A (Montana)
11. FLOR**IDA**; **IDA**HO
12. **JACK**SON (Mississippi)
13. **JEFF**ERSON CITY (Missouri)
14. **JUNE**AU (Alaska)
15. **KEN**TUCKY
16. **LOUIS**IANA
17. HONO**LULU** (Hawaii)
18. **MARY**LAND
19. ST. **PAUL** (Minnesota)
20. OLYM**PIA** (Washington)
21. **RICH**MOND (Virginia)
22. **SAL**EM (Oregon)
23. **TEX**AS
24. **TRENT**ON (New Jersey)
25. PENNSYL**VAN**IA
26. **WES**T VIRGINIA

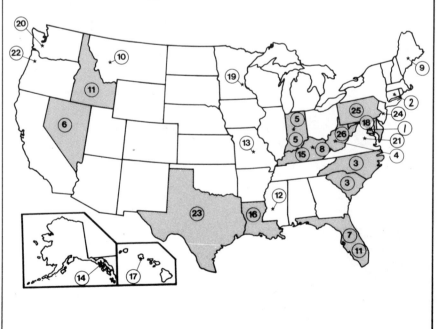

150 THREE-SUM

There are 13 triangles with dots totaling a multiple of three. Four of them are of the smallest size, six are the next size up, two are the size above that, and one is the entire triangle, which has 45 dots.

150 BREAK IT UP

1. dragon; drag on
2. me at; meat
3. pa rent; parent
4. cart on; carton
5. was her; washer
6. island; is land

151 FACTS AND FIGURES

1. 120	8. 42
2. 12	9. 20
3. 3	10. 28
4. 8	11. 87
5. 2	12. 8
6. 5	13. 10
7. 353	Total: 698

152 SEVEN UP!

1. V
2. I (Skiing is simply riding hills with thin sticks.)
3. C (A-4; B-1; C-5)
4. T
5. O (grid)

6. R (art)
7. Y The words: hottest; extra; battle; teeth; fall; phone. The sentence: The next to last letter of the alphabet.

The final word: VICTORY.